Llewellyn's

Witches' Datebook

2017

Featuring

Art by Kathleen Edwards
Text by Alaric Albertsson, Elizabeth Barrette,
Thuri Calafia, Monica Crosson, Ellen Dugan,
Ember Grant, Robin Ivy Payton,
Suzanne Ress, and Charlie Rainbow Wolf

ISBN 978-0-7387-3767-6

2017

JANUARY						
S	M	T	W	T	F	S
1	2	3	4	5	6	7
8	9	10	11	12	13	14
15	16	17	18	19	20	21
22	23	24	25	26	27	28
29	30	31				

FEBRUARY						
S	M	T	W	T	F	S
			1	2	3	4
5	6	7	8	9	10	11
12	13	14	15	16	17	18
19	20	21	22	23	24	25
26	27	28				

MARCH						
S	M	T	W	T	F	S
			1	2	3	4
5	6	7	8	9	10	11
12	13	14	15	16	17	18
19	20	21	22	23	24	25
26	27	28	29	30	31	

APRIL						
S	M	T	W	T	F	S
						1
2	3	4	5	6	7	8
9	10	11	12	13	14	15
16	17	18	19	20	21	22
23	24	25	26	27	28	29
30						

MAY						
S	M	T	W	T	F	S
	1	2	3	4	5	6
7	8	9	10	11	12	13
14	15	16	17	18	19	20
21	22	23	24	25	26	27
28	29	30	31			

JUNE						
S	M	T	W	T	F	S
				1	2	3
4	5	6	7	8	9	10
11	12	13	14	15	16	17
18	19	20	21	22	23	24
25	26	27	28	29	30	

JULY						
S	M	T	W	T	F	S
						1
2	3	4	5	6	7	8
9	10	11	12	13	14	15
16	17	18	19	20	21	22
23	24	25	26	27	28	29
30	31					

AUGUST						
S	M	T	W	T	F	S
		1	2	3	4	5
6	7	8	9	10	11	12
13	14	15	16	17	18	19
20	21	22	23	24	25	26
27	28	29	30	31		

SEPTEMBER						
S	M	T	W	T	F	S
					1	2
3	4	5	6	7	8	9
10	11	12	13	14	15	16
17	18	19	20	21	22	23
24	25	26	27	28	29	30

OCTOBER						
S	M	T	W	T	F	S
1	2	3	4	5	6	7
8	9	10	11	12	13	14
15	16	17	18	19	20	21
22	23	24	25	26	27	28
29	30	31				

NOVEMBER						
S	M	T	W	T	F	S
			1	2	3	4
5	6	7	8	9	10	11
12	13	14	15	16	17	18
19	20	21	22	23	24	25
26	27	28	28	30		

DECEMBER						
S	M	T	W	T	F	S
					1	2
3	4	5	6	7	8	9
10	11	12	13	14	15	16
17	18	19	20	21	22	23
24	25	26	27	28	29	30
31						

2018

JANUARY						
S	M	T	W	T	F	S
	1	2	3	4	5	6
7	8	9	10	11	12	13
14	15	16	17	18	19	20
21	22	23	24	25	26	27
28	29	30	31			

FEBRUARY						
S	M	T	W	T	F	S
				1	2	3
4	5	6	7	8	9	10
11	12	13	14	15	16	17
18	19	20	21	22	23	24
25	26	27	28			

MARCH						
S	M	T	W	T	F	S
				1	2	3
4	5	6	7	8	9	10
11	12	13	14	15	16	17
18	19	20	21	22	23	24
25	26	27	28	29	30	31

APRIL						
S	M	T	W	T	F	S
1	2	3	4	5	6	7
8	9	10	11	12	13	14
15	16	17	18	19	20	21
22	23	24	25	26	27	28
29	30					

MAY						
S	M	T	W	T	F	S
		1	2	3	4	5
6	7	8	9	10	11	12
13	14	15	16	17	18	19
20	21	22	23	24	25	26
27	28	29	30	31		

JUNE						
S	M	T	W	T	F	S
					1	2
3	4	5	6	7	8	9
10	11	12	13	14	15	16
17	18	19	20	21	22	23
24	25	26	27	28	29	30

JULY						
S	M	T	W	T	F	S
1	2	3	4	5	6	7
8	9	10	11	12	13	14
15	16	17	18	19	20	21
22	23	24	25	26	27	28
29	30	31				

AUGUST						
S	M	T	W	T	F	S
			1	2	3	4
5	6	7	8	9	10	11
12	13	14	15	16	17	18
19	20	21	22	23	24	25
26	27	28	29	30	31	

SEPTEMBER						
S	M	T	W	T	F	S
						1
2	3	4	5	6	7	8
9	10	11	12	13	14	15
16	17	18	19	20	21	22
23	24	25	26	27	28	29
30						

OCTOBER						
S	M	T	W	T	F	S
	1	2	3	4	5	6
7	8	9	10	11	12	13
14	15	16	17	18	19	20
21	22	23	24	25	26	27
28	29	30	31			

NOVEMBER						
S	M	T	W	T	F	S
				1	2	3
4	5	6	7	8	9	10
11	12	13	14	15	16	17
18	19	20	21	22	23	24
25	26	27	28	29	30	

DECEMBER						
S	M	T	W	T	F	S
						1
2	3	4	5	6	7	8
9	10	11	12	13	14	15
16	17	18	19	20	21	22
23	24	25	26	27	28	29
30	31					

Editing/design by Ed Day and Lauryn Heineman

Cover illustration and interior art © 2016 by Kathleen Edwards

Art on chapter openings © 2006 by Jennifer Hewitson

Art direction by Lynne Menturweck

Table of Contents

How to Use *Llewellyn's Witches' Datebook* 4
The Smile Inside *by Robin Ivy Payton* 6
Simple Amulet Pouches *by Charlie Rainbow Wolf* 10
The Hag Knows Best *by Suzanne Ress* 14
The Magic of Language *by Elizabeth Barrette* 19
Mending Energetic Fences *by Ellen Dugan* 24
January 28
February 38
March 46
April 55
May 64
June 72
July 81
August 90
September 98
October 107
November 116
December 124
About the Authors 134
Appendix 136
Notes 142

How to Use Llewellyn's Witches' Datebook

Welcome to *Llewellyn's Witches' Datebook 2017*! This datebook was designed especially for Witches, Pagans, and magical people. Use it to plan sabbat celebrations, magic, Full Moon rites, and even dentist and doctor appointments. At right is a symbol key to some of the features of this datebook.

MOON QUARTERS: The Moon's cycle is divided into four quarters, which are noted in the calendar pages along with their exact times. When the Moon changes quarter, both quarters are listed, as well as the time of the change. In addition, a symbol for the new quarter is placed where the numeral for the date usually appears.

MOON IN THE SIGNS: Approximately every two and a half days, the Moon moves from one zodiac sign to the next. The sign that the Moon is in at the beginning of the day (midnight Eastern Time) is noted next to the quarter listing. If the Moon changes signs that day, there will be a notation saying "☽ enters" followed by the symbol for the sign it is entering.

MOON VOID-OF-COURSE: Just before the Moon enters a new sign, it will make one final aspect (angular relationship) to another planet. Between that last aspect and the entrance of the Moon into the next sign it is said to be void-of-course. Activities begun when the Moon is void-of-course rarely come to fruition, or they turn out very differently than planned.

PLANETARY MOVEMENT: When a planet or asteroid moves from one sign into another, this change (called an *ingress*) is noted on the calendar pages with the exact time. The Moon and Sun are considered planets in this case. The planets (except for the Sun and Moon) can also appear to move backward as seen from the Earth. This is called a *planetary retrograde*, and is noted on the calendar pages with the symbol ℞. When the planet begins to move forward, or direct, again, it is marked D, and the time is also noted.

PLANTING AND HARVESTING DAYS: The best days for planting and harvesting are noted on the calendar pages with a seedling icon (planting) and a basket icon (harvesting).

TIME ZONE CHANGES: The times and dates of all astrological phenomena in this datebook are based on Eastern time. If you live outside the Eastern time zone, you will need to make the following changes: Pacific Time subtract three hours; Mountain Time subtract two hours; Central Time subtract one hour; Alaska subtract four hours; and Hawaii subtract five hours. All data is adjusted for Daylight Saving Time.

Planets

☉	Sun	♆	Neptune
☽	Moon	♇	Pluto
☿	Mercury	⚷	Chiron
♀	Venus	⚳	Ceres
♂	Mars	⚴	Pallas
♃	Jupiter	⚵	Juno
♄	Saturn	⚶	Vesta
♅	Uranus		

Signs

♈	Aries	♐	Sagittarius
♉	Taurus	♑	Capricorn
♊	Gemini	♒	Aquarius
♋	Cancer	♓	Pisces
♌	Leo		
♍	Virgo		
♎	Libra		
♏	Scorpio		

Motion

℞ Retrograde
D Direct

1st Quarter/New Moon ☽
2nd Quarter ☾

3rd Quarter/Full Moon ☺
4th Quarter ☽

☽ **Tuesday** ◄──────── Day and date
1st ♎ ◄──────────── Moon's quarter and sign
2nd Quarter 4:01 am ◄──── Moon quarter change
☽ v/c 4:01 am ◄──────── Moon void-of-course
☽ enters ♏ 9:30 am ◄──── Moon sign change/ingress
♄ ℞ 10:14 am ◄──────── Planetary retrograde
Color: Gray ◄────────── Color of the day

Planting day ──► 🌱

Harvesting day ──► 🧺

5

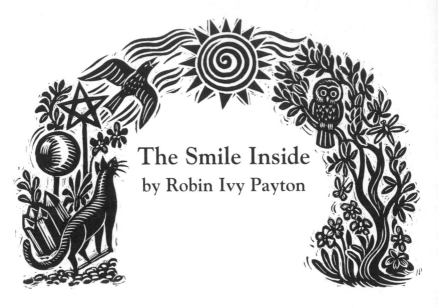

The Smile Inside
by Robin Ivy Payton

"We shall never know all the good that a simple smile can do."
—Mother Teresa

Your joyful expression reflects inner light, the way the Moon draws light from the Sun. Like the Moon, a smile appears crescent shaped though its wholeness exists beyond what's visible to the human eye. Take one deep breath right now, form a smile on your face, and notice how you feel. Chances are you respond on the inside and the outside. What happens with your breath, your eyes, and your mind? Even if you are completely forcing or faking, physical and mental effects are taking place. Try it one more time.

Your crescent-shaped smile is, in fact, a circular path. Most often induced by happy experiences like seeing a friend, watching pets and children play, or reading a heartwarming or amusing story, a smile radiates out, influences others, and is reflected back to you. The circular loop happens on an inner level as well. Information processed in the brain transmits neurons that tell the muscles of your face to smile. In more technical terms, a real smile is generated when both the zygomaticus major, the muscle controlling the corners of the mouth, and the orbicularis oculi, the muscles of the eye socket, activate. Then, magic happens! Not only does the brain tell the face to appear happy, the smile itself feeds happiness back to the brain, and good feelings expand. This circular path between the mind and the facial expression is a built-in reward mechanism and is powerful for reducing stress. "Feel good" hormones are secreted when you smile, even if you're faking it a little. Like sunshine, chocolate, exercise, and spicy foods, your smiling face leads to endorphin release and elevates your mood.

You've also undoubtedly noticed that smiles are contagious: when one person smiles, others smile back. It is true that smiling correlates to socializing and seems to happen more often in the presence of others. However, you can create a smile anytime you need it and send it deeper than the surface of your skin. Like all magic and manifestation, it's most potent when you focus only on your smile. Create a bit of time to smile at yourself before a job interview, date, or any situation that might create anxiety. Smile on the inside when things do not go as planned or, on the flip side, to celebrate success. You can even extend a loving smile throughout your physical and energetic body when someone has been negative or hurtful. Your very own smile helps with resilience as it bounces you back, gently combating any detrimental effects to your emotional well-being and stress level. Frequent practice may strengthen the happiness muscle.

A Smile Meditation

Perhaps you're wondering how one smiles at oneself. One way is to practice while looking in a mirror. Alternatively, with a deeper smile, you can extend through the systems of the body, the organs, all the connective tissues, and bones. It is an inner smile infusing you with friendliness and love toward yourself. This smile meditation is rooted in Taoist philosophy and has been written, recommended, and recreated over many years. This version is from me to you with a smile.

1. Begin by finding a comfortable spot where you feel secure and at ease enough to close your eyes. Sit or lie down, and just notice the feeling of the air on your skin and other pleasant sensory stimuli, such as birds singing, the sound of water moving, and the scents of flowers, food cooking, or sea air. Inhale and feel your chest, ribcage, and stomach move with the breath. Exhale fully and notice the natural contraction

in your body as you release all the air out. Take several cycles of this conscious breath, centering yourself. As you breathe, begin to withdraw from sensory input by letting the ears, mouth, and eyes rest. Rather than seeking or reaching out for sound, scent, or taste, settle inward and allow any of those things to move in and out without thinking, judging, or responding to them.

2. In this new awareness and presence you've created for yourself, imagine a time you are grateful for, a day or moment filled with joy and satisfaction. Fill in the details of this time, including the environment, people, animals, and all that was part of your experience. You might find yourself smiling. With this happy memory in mind, visualize a smile that starts behind your eyes, in the back of the mind. You might find this space midway between your ears in the center of the head. Breathe in and out slowly, continuing a steady rhythm. Let your inner smile take hold.

3. Picture your inner smile growing from ear to ear and lighting up around your eyes, forehead, cheeks, and jaw. When the smile fills your head, let it overflow to the upper spine, around the throat and neck. Perhaps your smile has color or shifts as it moves. Be open to the sensation, which may include feelings of wonder, amusement, or calm. As your smile continues to flow into your body, allow it to move across the clavicles, chest, and heart. The heart has a natural path into the shoulders, arms, hands, and fingers. Your entire upper body is now vibrating at a higher frequency, the level of optimism and healing.

4. Moving from the heart space, let your smile fall like water deep into the organs. Smile to your lungs, stomach, liver, and kidneys, and thank them for keeping you strong, nourished, and detoxified. Smile to the organs and tissues of the lower abdomen, including the pelvis, reproductive organs, bladder, and intestines. Let the spirit of your smile run down into the legs, where the energy paths called meridians extend into the ankles, feet, and toes. Bless every toe with your inner smile. Extend your loving gratitude to your own body, bones to flesh, for its consistent rhythm twenty-four hours a day.

5. Your inner smile may lead you to a natural state of peace where you can meditate awhile longer and resonate with the life force you've just created. Another option is to go back to the space behind your eyes and begin the inner smile again or even a third time for luck.

Applying Your Smile

When undergoing a medical procedure or surgery, practice the inner smile to prepare yourself. You can begin weeks or days before your appointment. Set aside a time of day, perhaps the time your surgery will occur, and engage in the smile from head to toe with special attention to the area of your body that needs healing. Thank the organs, muscles, and bones as you pass by them with your mind's smile. Before anesthesia or other preparation, smile again at yourself fully. This invisible meditation with breath can calm the nervous system and reassure you on a cellular level, especially if you've practiced in advance, training your nervous system to respond.

By imprinting yourself with a full-body smile, you become a friend to yourself. When someone smiles at you and you smile back, you sense approval and share a moment of common experience. With an inner smile, you can give yourself the same message: "I like you," "You're doing great," "Look how healthy and resilient you are," or "I appreciate you."

Finally, it may be useful to note that some people cannot control their facial smile because of illness, stroke, or nerve damage, for example. The inner smile is a potent tool to share with those who can't voluntarily smile. In many cases, they can smile in meditation, radiating happiness through the body. Generating positive feelings by practicing the smile might even increase their confidence or quality of life.

A genuine method of shapeshifting, the smile meditation works from the inside out. Relax as your cells rejuvenate with feelings of gratitude, love, and acceptance, and soon you may be showing a different face to the world. Like the Moon, your smile is always there waiting to fully light up.

Simple Amulet Pouches

by Charlie Rainbow Wolf

It is believed that from man's earliest days of awareness on this planet he has protected himself with some kind of amulet or talisman. An amulet has been defined as any object—usually worn around the neck—to which specific metaphysical powers have been ascribed. Throughout the years, the style and trend of amulets have changed with popular fashions, but their purpose has always endured. An amulet is as unique as the person for whom it is made. Whether it is for health or wealth, protection or empowerment, success or fertility, or just about any other need known to man, amulets have prevailed.

The New Moon is a good time to start making an amulet; the energies can grow as the Moon waxes. Have all the items that you want to use ready—not just the materials for the amulet pouch, but also the items you're going to include in it and any decoration you're going to put on it. Think about things like sharp scissors, a glover's needle or a hole punch if you're going to use an animal skin, or a needle and thread for cloth. Keep in mind that there's really no right or wrong way to do this. What matters is your intent.

Making the Amulet

Deerskin or other animal hide is a good choice for the pouch, although probably not for some vegetarians and vegans. Denim or heavy durable cotton would be suitable, as would any natural fabric. Although there is nothing wrong with man-made fabrics, you may prefer to work with more natural materials when making amulets and medicine pouches. Deerskin is popular because in many cultures, the deer represents gentleness. In *The Druid Animal Oracle*, Philip and Stephanie Carr-Gomm tell us that the hind represents subtlety and gracefulness, while the stag indicates independence and purification, other qualities that you want to embody in your amulet pouch.

Whatever material you choose, make sure that it resonates with you. I once knew someone who made amulets from his old leather jacket. He couldn't bear to part with the jacket because it was full of good energy and happy memories. Not only is this a very good illustration of the importance of making something with intent, it is also an excellent example of recycling.

Before using your chosen material, it's a good idea to make a paper template. This will help you get the dimensions of your amulet right. Usually a U shape of approximately 3 inches wide and 4 inches high suffices; this makes a nice-sized, small pouch and allows for a seam. A fabric pouch will have to be cut slightly taller than a hide pouch to allow for a top hem so that there is a casing through which the thonging can be threaded. Using a fine ballpoint pen, lightly draw around the paper pattern onto the back side of your chosen material. Two pieces will be required, one for each side of the pouch. You might want to cut out any fringe or other adornments at this time, too.

You'll also want to cut a neck cord if the pouch is to be worn around the neck. Leather thonging or thread is a good choice for this, but other materials can be used, too. Make sure that the length of the cord is long enough to be threaded through the amulet and knotted. I recommend adding an extra inch or so for good measure. The cord can always be cut to length when construction is finished, but it can be frustrating to finish the amulet only to find it won't fit over your head!

If you're using hide, then it is time to mark the placement of the holes for sewing. Using a needle, awl, or even a pen, mark one piece of the hide where the hole punches are going to go. Space them evenly around the pouch, about ¼ to ½ inch apart, and keep the top open for the time being. Then, use a hole punch set on a smallish setting and position a piece of scrap hide underneath the pouch sides to ensure a clean cut. Line up the top and the bottom of your hide and punch the holes in both pieces of the pouch at once, taking care not to get too near the edges. Punching through both pieces of the hide at the same time aligns the holes for sewing. If using woven material as opposed to hide, it is best to sew the pouch with a needle and thread using a running stitch. Turn down the top hem after the side seams have been sewn, and don't forget to leave an opening at the center back for the thonging.

With front sides facing, use the piece of leather lacing and work with a blanket stitch or a whipstitch. Oversew the two pieces of hide together through the holes that were punched. Secure the ends underneath the stitching at the beginning and the end of the sewing. Now use the hole punch again and punch four holes at equal intervals about ¾ inch from the top edge of the amulet. You might want to mark them before cutting to make sure you get them even. Then punch them as before, with the scrap of leather underneath.

If you'd prefer to just sew the hide, then a glover's needle is required. This has a slight cutting edge to the point, making it easier to pierce through the animal hide. Using artificial sinew will give the sewing strength, but nylon thread is strong too.

Filling the Amulet

The amulet is now ready to be filled. Keep in mind that you want your amulet to tell your story, to contain things that are magical or meaningful to you. The actual value of the articles in the pouch is not important—what matters is why they are important. You might want to add things like your birthstone, a pebble collected after a special ceremony, or a token given to you by someone special. Amulets such as these are not collections of items; they are collections of experiences.

Once the amulet has been filled, tie it shut. Lacing from the same hide or material as the body of the amulet can be used, or a waxed cotton thread might also be threaded through the holes. Start from the center back and, working through single layers of the hide, weave in and out to the center front. If a pendant or bead or other item is desired at the front of the amulet, add it here. Continue to thread the lacing through the holes and around to the back again, then tie it closed with a square knot. This ensures that you can untie it and add other items to your amulet at a later time as you grow on your path. Tie the other ends of the lacing in an overhand knot, and the amulet is now ready.

Variations

Larger medicine bundles or crane bags can be made in a similar way. The hunters and traders of eighteenth-century America called these "possibles bags" because you carried with you everything you might possibly need. Just like amulets, these can be made from a variety of materials, although they may need to be more durable than your amulet. Hide is a good choice, as is denim, canvas, or broadcloth.

Construct the bag to be large enough to hold the objects you wish to put into it and also large enough that you can comfortably reach your hand into it to retrieve things. Making the bag with the amulet method but using a larger pattern is a good place to start. Gather your materials before starting—it's very annoying to have to make a mad dash to the store once you're in the middle of the construction! The decoration can be as basic or as elaborate as you choose. The idea is to have the bag reflect its usage. You may want to put something on there to represent a season, or a deity, or some other kind of affiliation.

Once your bag is finished, simply fill it. These items do not need to be as intimate as the ones that went into your personal medicine pouch or amulet. The small amulet that you made to wear is a personal contract between you and the universe; the larger bag is more like a toolbelt.

As you progress with making these little pouches and larger bags, you might like to experiment with different inclusions, different patterns, and different materials. See how the energies feel when comparing deerskin to cowhide or pigskin. Make them at different phases of the Moon and notice the different changes in the way you relate to them. Put different decorations on them: paint one, do beadwork on another, leave yet another one plain. As stated previously, there really is no right or wrong way to make these; it is the intent that is all-important.

The Hag Knows Best

by Suzanne Ress

Being called a "hag" is not usually considered a compliment. The word carries connotations of being old, ugly, willful, ill-tempered, easily angered, contemptuous, and, of course, it can only be applied to women. There really is no masculine equivalent.

In pre-Christian times, societies regarded the postmenopausal hag woman as a fiercely wise, independent being with close connections to the spirit world. Hags were experienced, knowledgeable truth-tellers and soothsayers whose counsel on many matters was sought after by men and women from all walks of life.

The word "hag," which derives from the same root as the German word *hexe* (witch), was used in prepatriarchal times to indicate a woman who lived outside the fray, or "in the hedge." She was powerful; dealt with nature, herbs, and potions; and could do magic. She was feared and respected.

Nowadays sometimes the words "hag" and "witch" are used interchangeably, but in a derogatory sense, as in "an ugly, nasty, old woman you'd be better off avoiding." All the magic, sacredness, and respect have been taken away, and I think it is time to put them back!

Historic and Modern-Day Hags

Hags have been around for a very long time. The Greek Moon goddess Hecate, who originally represented the female trinity of virgin, mother, and crone, became best known in her crone or hag form, as goddess of the underworld. Hecate is a death goddess and a deity of magic and prophecy. She rules over midwives and is invoked by travelers before setting out on a journey. In her role as a death goddess, the hag Hecate was also a priestess of sacrifice, who, presumably, preferred her victims chopped into little pieces: both haggis, the Scot-

tish chopped meat specialty, and British hash, made of finely chopped meat, are considered hag's dishes, as their names declare.

It has become normal in modern times to deny (at least concerning humans and their pets) that death is a necessary part of the life cycle. We seek to extend life as long as possible and mourn the passing even of very old, sick, worn-out beings. But consider for a moment a tree's foliage. The leaves bud early in the spring; they unfurl and the tree's flowers bloom, are pollinated, and turn into seeds, nuts, or fruit. By late autumn, everything has shriveled, dried up, and fallen to the ground, dead. As the dead leaves and husks decompose, they serve as nutrients for new, young trees, and so the cycle continues. Without the death of the old, there can be no new life, no virgins, and no mothers. The hag and death are necessary and important.

The hag is also a stock character in fairy tales. Some of the most well-known fairy tale hags are Hansel and Gretel's witch, Rapunzel's enchantress, and Snow White's stepmother.

In Hansel and Gretel, the witch/hag welcomes the cold, hungry, tired children into her cottage, feeds them well, and puts them comfortably to bed. Only when the children realize that the hag intends to eat them do they suddenly come to their senses and, for the first time in the story, behave intelligently, acting together to kill the hag and find their way back home. Without the hag's help, they would have perished—instead, they return home stronger and wiser than they were when they left.

Rapunzel's enchantress/hag isolates her in a tower where she is well cared for but lonely. Rapunzel deceives the hag by planning to escape with the prince. The hag, in her fury, sends the newly pregnant Rapunzel into the desert and blinds the prince. Only after a long, wretched

period of suffering (Rapunzel's twins are at least four years old by then) does Rapunzel meet her blinded prince once again. Her tears of joy restore his sight, and the family returns to his castle to live happily ever after. But without the years of wretched suffering in the desert, during which the two young lovers independently discover their own strengths and capabilities, the happy ending could not have occurred.

When Snow White's beautiful stepmother discovers that Snow White is still alive and living with the dwarfs, she transforms herself into the hag and attempts to lure Snow White to her death with pretty trinkets (the asphyxiating laces, the poisoned comb, and the poisoned apple), and, on the third try, she succeeds. Snow White, the virgin, is then born again at the prince's kiss, with the implied promise of motherhood, just as the stepmother/hag dies of envy and rage to complete the cycle.

In many fairy and folk tales the pattern goes like this: The hag creates a block or barrier to the hero or heroine's goal. Then she sets a series, usually three, of seemingly impossible tests that the hero must successfully complete in order to overcome the barrier. The tests are really there to develop the hero's ability to discriminate between truth and falsehood, his patience, and his ability to surrender himself to the spirit. With the help of supernatural animals or other beings, the hero manages to pass the first two tests but fails the third. The hag, seeing that the hero has sufficiently developed his sense of self, has mercy and takes away the barrier anyway. Soon after, the hag often transforms back into the virgin.

These hags of fairy and folk tales, who represent true hagdom, are not sweet old ladies! They are dangerous and radical, ruled by no one but themselves. Hags are terrifying forces to be reckoned with, but if one is courageous enough to undergo their tests and willing to accept their counsel, they can be merciful and kind. In the end, an encounter with a hag strengthens a person's psyche and sense of self-worth, even when the truth is hard to take.

Listen to Your Inner Hag

Hag magic is not just for old women. Symbolically, a hag is the third and final stage of the feminine side of anyone's psychic development. She represents completeness and is a necessary step in self-realization. We can all access our inner hag, regardless of age or sex.

Your inner hag is the rebellious, possibly cranky, and obstinate voice inside you that utters truths you would often rather not listen to. Start paying more attention to her. Offer her a bigger part in your life—if you dare!

Do you have fair-weather friends who seem to be taking advantage of you? Let your hag tell them what you really feel. You have nothing to lose. Has a family member asked for your advice about a relationship? Let your hag speak up—tell the truth without being mean, even if the truth may hurt. The family member will likely end up thanking you for it. But your hag already knows that. Often, when asked her opinion, a hag will reply with a truth-revealing question, such as, "Well, how would you like me to answer that?"

Exercises

The following are some specific exercises and spells one can do to get in touch with and amplify one's inner hag.

Take out the Nine of Swords from a deck of tarot cards. It depicts the end of a nightmare or overcoming the tests, and the moment of understanding. Spend time contemplating this card every day for seven days.

Visualize yourself standing before the most terrifying hag imaginable. She sets three tests for you. What are these? Imagine, in great detail and at length, the hardships you encounter while attempting to pass these tests in order to reach your goal. Continue this visualization for as long as necessary to remove any blocks you have.

Create a shrine to the hag. Decorate it with images of cats, black dogs, skulls, cauldrons, and fire. Carve the triple goddess symbol into a black candle, but only burn this in darkness. Ask the hag for assistance in matters involving the psyche and the spirit.

Have a Hecate Supper at a three-way crossroads. Prepare a fine meal that includes fish, garlic, honey, lavender or rosemary, and whatever else you deem appropriate. After dark take this meal to a three-way crossroads somewhere quiet, perhaps out in the country. If weather and other conditions permit, sit down at the crossroads and dine with Hecate. Otherwise, leave the meal for her, plate and all, and do not turn back.

Spells

Plants of genus *Artemisia* can be put to use in calling on the hag. The Greek goddess Artemis, who sometimes assumes hag form, rules over magic, the psyche, and wild female nature. Soften a sprig of wormwood or mugwort in a bottle of red wine, make a tea of dried mugwort or wormwood, or make or buy a bottle of absinthe. Take small sips of your chosen *Artemisia* beverage while doing your spellwork. (Do not use any of these if you are pregnant!)

Spells invoking the hag can be done at the Full Moon or during the last quarter. Use only black or white candles, and focus on the image of a powerful, intuitive, old woman who is pleased to walk alone.

The Magic of Language

by Elizabeth Barrette

Language is one of the major avenues to magic. We use it in spells, chants, mantras, liturgy, and many other applications. Most of us work magic in our everyday language. However, some people use a different language for their magical/spiritual work. Other times, they use their everyday language but write it in a mystical alphabet. Some magical alphabets have their own uses in spellcraft as well.

These approaches offer multiple benefits. One is that using a mystical language clearly distinguishes conversation from spellcraft. You don't have to worry about a spell going off at random. This relates to the use of certain activation phrases in rituals: "So mote it be!" serves much the same purpose as "Run program." Another benefit is that it adds power. Your mind learns that speaking or writing a mystical language means that it's time to work magic now. Over time, this builds intensity. Finally, you enjoy more secrecy for your work. This is a key reason why magical alphabets are popular; you don't have to learn a whole new language, just a new writing system, and then most people can't read your Book of Shadows. That's a good thing if you have nosy relatives.

Let's look at some options for magical languages and alphabets.

Whole Languages

The world contains thousands of languages. Some of these have a close association with magic and Paganism. This can be because they developed a distinct tradition of their own or because other folks have

borrowed the language for their own uses. Sometimes when we explore historic artifacts, we find traces of the spells and rituals that people recorded.

The Egyptian language is old enough that it evolved over time through several stages, including Archaic, Old, Middle, Late, Demotic, and Coptic Egyptian. That span runs from before 2600 BCE through the present day. Egyptian has also used multiple writing systems. Hieroglyphs are the most famous, but there are also hieratic, Demotic, and Coptic—plus it's sometimes written in Arabic lettering today. Hieroglyphs (or in Egyptian, *mdw·w-nṯr*, "god's words") included logographic and alphabetic elements, meaning the pictures could represent the things they showed or a specific sound instead. Hieratic means "priestly writing" and it was used only for religious purposes. It developed alongside the more detailed hieroglyphs and could be written faster.

The vocabulary of Egyptian is useful if you practice Khemetic magic; the *neteru* (deities) appreciate hearing followers speak the religion's native tongue. Hieroglyphs are popular in jewelry and other artifacts; it's fairly easy to find a set of stamps to make them. Surviving documents indicate that they were used extensively in Egyptian spellcasting and charms. Just make sure you know what you're writing!

The earliest written examples of Hebrew date from around 900 BCE. As a spoken language, it flourished from approximately 1200 to 586 BCE. Somewhere between 200 to 400 CE, it became dormant as an everyday language, surviving only in liturgical use. Then Hebrew did something that few languages have ever achieved: in the late 1800s to early 1900s it revived as a spoken language, and today it has many speakers. It is read from right to left.

Speaking and writing Hebrew helps the most if you practice Qabala. The words frame ideas particular to Semitic culture, religion, and magic. The squarish alphabet is popular for calligraphy and for writing spells. Each letter has its own symbolism. You can often find them on jewelry or other crafts.

Latin is interesting because it relates to two completely different religious and magical systems: Roman Paganism and Christianity. Latin developed through the stages of Old Latin, Classical Latin and Vulgar Latin (at the same time), Medieval Latin, Renaissance Latin, Early Modern Latin, and Modern Latin. Between about 501 and 900 CE, it also spawned the whole family of Romance languages, including modern Italian, Spanish, and French.

Because of its historic uses, Latin works great for both Roman Pagans and Christo-Pagans. Its formal structure is particularly suited to the "contract magic" practiced in Roman temples where a follower would stipulate certain offerings in exchange for specific boons from a god or goddess. People also associate it with formality, making it a logical choice for ceremonial magic—and indeed it appears in many ceremonial traditions and secret societies.

Writing Systems

Magical writing systems may be connected with a native language, or they may be substitutions for a more common alphabet. They are useful for several reasons. One is that you can encode your thoughts without having to learn a whole new language, just the new shapes. Another is that the symbols often have their own magical meaning, which makes them ideal to use on magical artifacts.

The Norse runes have been used to write Old Norse and a few other languages, with the earliest inscriptions appearing around 150 CE. The Elder Futhark has twenty-four runes in angular shapes, divided into three *ættir* of eight runes each. They appear throughout much of Europe on artifacts such as standing stones, swords, and torcs. They may be written horizontally or vertically, and are read from left to right. Runecraft involves using the runes to cast spells, with each rune having its own qualities.

Among the traditional uses are runestaves and bindrunes. A runestave is a post with one or more runes carved into it and displayed to mark or protect land. A bindrune consists of several runes linked together to form a new shape, combining their powers. Runes may also be placed on disks or dice for use in divination. They are customarily carved into wood

and painted red. That's why all the lines are straight—it's hard to carve rounded lines across the grain.

The Ogham alphabet comes from the Druids, and has been used to write various Celtic languages. They take the form of hashmarks against or through a central line. Each letter in the Ogham relates to a tree or plant, sharing the same initial, so they're a little different across the languages. There are also dozens of other Ogham sets in everything from colors to birds—ancient mnemonics both for the vocabulary and the writing system itself. These associations lend themselves very well to magic. Ogham may be written vertically or horizontally. The earliest inscriptions date from the 300s, and it remained in use until around 1000 CE.

This writing system can be very discreet because it doesn't really look like an alphabet unless you know exactly what you are looking at; it looks like a set of numbered tallies. Ogham also works for putting names or charms onto magical artifacts. Individual Ogham symbols can evoke the properties of their associated tree, animal, or other concept. Sets of them are often used for divination, and you can combine sets from different tables of correspondence.

The Theban alphabet is said to come from Honorius of Thebes. The earliest known example dates from 1531 in *Three Books of Occult Philosophy* by Heinrich Cornelius Agrippa. Some people call it the Witch's Alphabet or the Runes of Honorius. The letters have a lot of hooks and curves, and the line width typically varies. They are meant to be written with a quill or calligraphy nib, and they look quite beautiful in that style. Witches most often use the Theban alphabet to encode a book of shadows, write spells, or label magical tools.

The Enochian alphabet by John Dee and Edward Kelley dates from visions beginning on March 26, 1583. It is written from right to left. The letters consist of lines and curves with strong variation in line width, meant to be written with a quill or calligraphy nib. This script is essential to the practice of Enochian magic, a ceremonial tradition concerned with summoning, controlling, and banishing various types of spirits.

The Angelic script was created by Heinrich Cornelius Agrippa some time in the 1500s. This is sometimes called the Celestial Alphabet—a term also used as a synonym for the Enochian alphabet, which is not the same script. The Angelic script has a distinctive appearance because the thin lines and curves are punctuated by small dots or circles at the ends. This makes it very popular for jewelry, as the dots can be marked with gems. It is sometimes used for writing in a Book of Shadows, but is most popular for spellcraft in ceremonial traditions that use angelic powers.

Anyone can add a magical language or writing system to their practice. As you can see from these examples, each one has its own unique features that suit it for particular purposes. So think about what you'd like to explore. Latin is a nice, flexible language that suits a lot of traditions and uses. Ogham and runes are good for Hedgecraft, while Enochian and Angelic are good for ceremonial traditions. Theban is among the most popular for secret writings. Of course, there are many more options besides these; they're just among the best known. Pick one and give it a try!

Mending Energetic Fences

by Ellen Dugan

Don't ever take a fence down until you know why it was put up.
—Ascribed to G. K. Chesterton by J. F. Kennedy

This summer we had to rebuild a massive section of our old privacy fence that protected one side of our home and our gardens. The original fence was over fifty feet in length and had held up for more than twenty years. That six-foot-tall cedar fence had had everything thrown at it in two decades: a few crazy next door neighbors, local miscreants, tornadoes, straight-line winds, blizzards, ice storms, my own teenagers—you name it. Through all of that, with only minor repairs and a whole lot of magick from me, it had stood the test of time. But we knew the whole thing needed to be torn down and built fresh. So this year we tackled the rebuild of the longest section of the original privacy fence, including the gate, ourselves. It wasn't until I took down my Green Man plaques, wind chimes, and assorted garden decorations from the inside of our old fence in advance of tearing it down that I realized just how much I had depended on that privacy fence, energetically.

Over the years I had found numerous ways to enchant the fence, which served as a barrier against the mundane outside world and a marker for the borders of my bewitching gardens. The privacy fence was a physical reminder and symbol of the area that I had designated as my own sacred space. Regarding energy, that privacy fence had soaked up a lot of "juice" over the years, from the happy energy raised by my family, to the magick and positive energy purposefully conjured and raised by my coven and various magickal friends.

The original privacy fence was cedar, and initially I had tapped into the classic attributes of that wood, which include protection, purification, and prosperity. Back then, my children were small and the gardens brand new when we first contracted and hired a company to build the fence.

At the time, the house next to us was a rental property, and the neighbors were a horrific nightmare. The police were constantly being called for domestic violence issues or disturbing the peace complaints. It later dawned on us that they were selling drugs out of that house. Imagine living in a nice little neighborhood with your grade-school children and having that right next door.

The six-foot-tall cedar fence became a priority in order to shield us from any garbage that the next-door neighbors might spew both physically and energetically. The fence allowed my children to enjoy their time in the yard again, gave us security and privacy to enjoy our gardens, and created a physical symbol—an energetic line drawn in the sand. The classic you-shall-not-pass, wizard-facing-down-a-monster type of thing. And, baby, did it work.

As I recall, the problematic neighbors moved out shortly after our fence went up. What followed for the next twenty years was a smorgasbord of families and retired couples but none of the horrible problems we'd faced before the fence was built.

To keep the energy of the garden on track and to reinforce the magickal border that protected our home, on every Full Moon I was out there working in the gardens and adding another energetic layer of security magick to the privacy fence. I would trail my hand along the boards, chanting spells quietly as a refresher once a month.

I call upon the powers of earth, fire, water, and wind
To protect my home and reinforce this privacy fence.

The fence soaked it up, and I bet that was one of the reasons it stood a good ten years longer than expected. Another charm I often worked when I was trying to keep any local troublemakers away from our property was this little ditty:

> My six-foot-tall fence built of cedar boards,
> Protect my home from the ravaging hoards.
> If troublemakers should approach my privacy fence,
> May their bad luck double and their fears grow immense.
> By the light of the Sun and Moon, this spell is spun.
> As I will, so mote it be; the magick is begun.

Yes, it is slightly dramatic and definitely tongue in cheek, but it always made me laugh. And sometimes a bit of laughter while you are casting adds an extra bit of oomph to your spells. Also, this spell doesn't play. If you choose to use it to mark the boundaries of your own yard and to turn a physical fence into an energetic fence, then keep in mind that a bit of snarky humor on your end can help keep the manifesting magick firm—but not cruel.

This summer, as I helped haul cedar posts and fence panels down to the bottom of our yard where we could recycle that old wood, I began to recall all of the old spells and charms I'd conjured up over the years. Perhaps it was a sort of postcognitive, clairtangent recollection. Postcognition is defined as gathering psychic information from the past, whereas clairtangency is the technical term for the ability of reading an object by placing your hands on it.

As the memories of past spells and charms swirled around me, I was upbeat and looking forward to the building of a pretty new fence that I had envisioned. However, once the posts, panels, and the gate were torn out, what was left was shocking.

The house and yard were completely open to view, and I admit after twenty-plus years of privacy, it made me very uneasy to leave the side yard and gardens exposed to the public eye. We live in an old, established suburb, and the houses around us range in age from fifty to one hundred years old. It was odd strolling out my back door to work in the gardens and realizing I was on display to anyone walking or driving down the street. Naturally, people were curious when we began the project, and folks were shocked to see our established perennial gardens that had been hidden behind the fence. And for several days many people wanted to come and take a look at them.

But I had become accustomed to, and counted on, the protection and privacy that the fence had provided. I stood under the moonlight that first night after the tear-out, in plain view of anyone walking along the street, and suddenly real-ized why I felt so uneasy. All of the magick that had built up in the old six-foot-tall privacy fence was now gone.

Or so I thought.

The next weekend when we began to set new fence posts in place, one of my neighbor's small children walked across his front yard and stopped dead at the line where the fence once stood. He

wanted to see the flowers, so I gestured for him to come over. To my shock, instead of walking forward through the grass to me, he literally walked all the way around and went over to the spot where the gate used to be— almost as if the fence were still in place. While his parents chuckled at the way he walked in, his little sister did exactly the same thing. Neither of the children would pass through the energetic boundary that had held for over twenty years.

It gave me quite a jolt to see a four-year-old instinctively know that there was still a barrier in place, even though the physical fence was gone. My husband slanted me a look as we visited with our cute little neighbors for a few moments. A short time later our visitors left, and we got down to work.

Two days later, our garden gate and privacy fence were rebuilt with the help of our sons and future son-in-law. It looked so pretty and fresh out there as we set the gardens right. That first night I hustled out to my gardens and charmed the new privacy fence. I felt the magick click back into place so easily that it caught me off guard. I realized that while the boards and posts were new, the energetic fence was very much still in place.

In closing, here is the spell that I used to reenchant and reactivate the energetic fence:

New posts of cedar and tall boards of pine
Now enchant and protect this home of mine.
Add a layer of magick with the words I weave;
An energetic fence, there shall now always be.
With my words, an old magick is made brand new.
May my family be blessed in all that we do.

26 Monday

4th ♐
Color: White

27 Tuesday

4th ♐
♀ enters ♓ 7:23 pm
☽ v/c 8:45 pm
Color: Black

Altar bells may be made of any sweet-toned material, such as brass, bronze, silver, or even glass. They banish negativity.

28 Wednesday

4th ♍
☽ enters ♑ 10:12 am
Color: Yellow

29 Thursday

4th ♑
New Moon 1:53 am
♅ D 4:29 am
Color: Turquoise

30 Friday

1st ♑
☽ v/c 3:07 am
☽ enters ♒ 8:29 pm
Color: Rose

Birch brings feminine power, based on the Moon and water. Its oil works well for fertility and birth ceremonies.

Snowflake Obsidian

Obsidian is often called volcanic glass due to its origins—when lava meets water, it cools so quickly that the atoms are not arranged into an ordered structure like other crystals. Obsidian is made mainly of silica, like quartz, and often contains other minerals. In snowflake obsidian, a mineral called cristobalite forms the distinctive white patterns that look like snowflakes.

Snowflake obsidian corresponds with the element of fire and the planet Saturn, so it's an excellent transformation stone. Helping you focus both your inner and outer vision, it enables you to break unnecessary patterns. Other metaphysical traits are grounding and shielding. During meditation, it can help reach a state of balance and serenity. It has been called a stone of purity.

Are you stuck in a rut? Feeling out of balance? Take advantage of this combination of contrasting black and white to break feelings of stagnation. Charge your stone with these words:

Keep me grounded as I grow—yin and yang, heat and snow.
Unity of dark and light, keep me balanced day and night.

—Ember Grant

---

31 Saturday

1st ≈
Color: Blue

New Year's Eve

---

1 Sunday

1st ≈
Color: Orange

New Year's Day
Kwanzaa ends
Hanukkah ends

---

2 Monday

1st ≈
☽ v/c 2:59 am
☽ enters ♓ 4:57 am
Color: Lavender

Andumbulu is an African underworld god
who rules alongside his brother Yeban.

3 Tuesday

1st ♓
♀ enters ♓ 2:47 am
Color: White

Salt water in a bowl purifies sacred space, connecting it with water.

4 Wednesday

1st ♓
☿ enters ♐ 9:17 am
☽ v/c 11:14 am
☽ enters ♈ 11:20 am
Color: Brown

◐ Thursday

1st ♈
2nd quarter 2:47 pm
Color: Purple

6 Friday

2nd ♈
☽ v/c 1:41 pm
☽ enters ♉ 3:18 pm
Color: Pink

Twelfth Night/Epiphany

Set in Eastern Standard Time (EST)

Æfterra Geōla (Late Yule)

In the Old English calendar, the first month following the winter solstice was called Late Yule or After Yule (*Æfterra Geōla*). Today many Pagans celebrate Yule as the solstice itself, but Yule used to be a full season, lasting through two lunar months. This latter month, Late Yule, was a time to prepare for the coming spring. Farmers once blessed their plows at a festival that came to be known, in the Christian era, as Plow Monday.

Most villages shared a common plow, which was stored in the local church when not in use. On the first Monday after Twelfth Day (January 6) a priest would bless the plow to ensure a divine sanction on the coming growing season. A text recorded in the eleventh century gives instructions for blessing a plow with frankincense, fennel, and salt.

You probably do not have a plow to bless, but this is a good time to reconsecrate your athame and other ritual tools. If you are a gardener, clean and repair the spades, hoes, and forks you use to work the soil. These can then be blessed by rubbing them with fennel and salt and passing them through frankincense fumes rising from your censer.

—Alaric Albertsson

---

7 Saturday

2nd ♉
☽ v/c 9:23 pm
Color: Indigo

Frankincense balances masculine and feminine energies. It matches the Sun, air, and fire. Use it as a sacred offering.

---

8 Sunday

2nd ♉
☿ D 4:43 am
☽ enters ♊ 5:06 pm
Color: Amber

Mercury direct (retrograde began December 19, 2016)

---

9 Monday
2nd ♊
Color: Gray

Vairocana is the Tibetan wisdom god who sits in the middle of a mandala.

10 Tuesday
2nd ♊
⚳ enters ♋ 1:11 pm
☽ v/c 4:38 pm
☽ enters ♋ 5:49 pm
Color: Black

A good example is the best enchantment.

11 Wednesday
2nd ♋
Color: Yellow

☺ Thursday
2nd ♋
☽ v/c 6:34 am
Full Moon 6:34 am
☿ enters ♑ 9:03 am
☽ enters ♌ 7:08 pm
Color: Crimson

Cold Moon

13 Friday
3rd ♌
Color: Rose

14 Saturday

3rd ♌
☽ v/c 10:17 am
☽ enters ♍ 10:52 pm
Color: Brown

15 Sunday

3rd ♍
Color: Gold

The wand, a rod typically made of wood or
metal, channels God energy to direct.

16 Monday
3rd ♍
Color: Silver

Martin Luther King Jr. Day

17 Tuesday
3rd ♍
☽ v/c 1:09 am
☽ enters ♎ 6:16 am
Color: Maroon

In 1904, the Ordo Templi Orientis was founded.

18 Wednesday
3rd ♎
Color: White

◑ Thursday
3rd ♎
☽ v/c 3:55 am
☉ enters ♒ 4:24 pm
☽ enters ♏ 5:09 pm
4th quarter 5:13 pm
Color: Turquoise

Sun enters Aquarius

20 Friday
4th ♏
Color: Coral

Inauguration Day

Corina's Greek Yogurt Pancakes

6 oz. of Greek yogurt
1 egg
Scant ½ cup flour
1 tsp. baking soda

The light is visibly stronger, and there is the scent of new earth on the breeze. The upcoming Imbolc is the time we celebrate the Goddess as she transforms from crone to maiden. And because traditional dishes include dairy, I thought it was appropriate to include this wonderful dish by Corina of Marblemount Homestead.

Put the yogurt in a bowl and crack an egg over it. Stir to combine. In a separate bowl, mix together the flour and baking soda. Pour yogurt and egg mixture into the bowl with the flour and baking soda. Stir to combine. The batter will be extremely thick. Spoon the batter onto a sprayed griddle or pan heated to medium-high. This recipe makes 4 big pancakes, but you could also make 8 smaller ones. Flip the pancakes when they start to bubble a bit on the surface. Cook until golden brown on both sides and serve with maple syrup, butter, honey, and fruit.

—Monica Crosson

21 Saturday

4th ♏
☽ v/c 8:24 pm
Color: Blue

Celtic Tree Month of Rowan begins

22 Sunday

4th ♏
☽ enters ♐ 5:45 am
Color: Yellow

23 Monday
4th ♐
Color: Ivory

A ring around the Moon forecasts rain within three days.

24 Tuesday
4th ♐
☽ v/c 12:33 pm
☽ enters ♑ 5:43 pm
Color: Gray

25 Wednesday
4th ♑
Color: Topaz

Globe amaranth is feminine, associated with Saturn and earth. It soothes emotional loss.

26 Thursday
4th ♑
Color: Green

Rowan is a fey tree that grants healing and strength.

☽ Friday
4th ♑
☽ v/c 2:18 am
☽ enters ♒ 3:37 am
New Moon 7:07 pm
Color: Purple

Hematite

Hematite is a metallic iron ore. Its name comes from the Greek *haima*, meaning "blood-like," due to the stone's red streak; it's also red in powdered form. This stone is believed to help one succeed in battle. Also, with a mirror-like luster, it is used for scrying.

Hematite is associated with the element of fire and the planet Saturn. It has a trigonal crystal structure, giving it forceful energy combined with balance. Metaphysically, hematite can be used to improve mental performance and technical skills. It's also useful for transforming negativity, achieving balance and self-control, and improving memory. It can balance emotions and help you transcend limitations.

When facing a task that demands your very best performance, carry or wear hematite. Visualize your body, mind, and spirit becoming aligned and know that these facets will work together to enable your best presentation. Chant these words to empower the stone and yourself:

Actions of the body, functions of the mind—
Movement with precision, synchronous design.

—Ember Grant

---

28 Saturday

1st ≈
♂ enters ♈ 12:39 am
Color: Black

Lunar New Year (Rooster)

---

29 Sunday

1st ≈
☽ v/c 12:52 am
☽ enters ♓ 11:10 am
Color: Orange

---

30 Monday
1st ♓
Color: White

White evokes space but also emptiness; break it up
with other colors to set the theme of altars or rooms.

31 Tuesday
1st ♓
☽ v/c 12:36 pm
☽ enters ♈ 4:46 pm
Color: Scarlet

1 Wednesday
1st ♈
Color: Brown

2 Thursday
1st ♈
☽ v/c 11:50 am
☽ enters ♉ 8:50 pm
Color: Crimson

Imbolc
Groundhog Day

☽ Friday
1st ♉
⚡ enters ♑ 1:47 am
♀ enters ♈ 10:51 am
2nd quarter 11:19 pm
Color: Rose

Imbolc crossquarter day
(Sun reaches 15° Aquarius)

Imbolc

Imbolc, the festival of light, is also often referred to as Brigid's Day. Brigid (pronounced "breed") is the Celtic goddess of healing, smithcraft, and poetry. She was turned into St. Bridget with the Christianization of Europe, but her worship has never died—her sacred wells can still be found in abundance throughout the Irish countryside, and at the great monastery in Kildare, her fire is still tended by nuns, never allowed to go out.

We can celebrate and honor her by weaving solar crosses out of craft straw, blessing water to bathe in or sprinkle our homes in purification, or making candles with magical intentions. Rolled beeswax candles are easy to make, and the colored wax can be layered with magical oils or herbs (not too many, or the herbs will blaze up like Roman candles!), imbuing the candle with our intentions. We can also purchase small, colored candles from metaphysical shops and inscribe them before dressing them with magical oils. A nice tradition is to dress (or make) a candle for each person we wish to send health, abundance, or other blessings to. It's best to get permission first or to ask their guardian spirit to only accept the blessing if the person desires it.

—Thuri Calafia

---

4 Saturday

2nd ☓
☽ v/c 5:42 pm
♀ enters ☓ 7:17 pm
☽ enters ♊ 11:44 pm
Color: Gray

Fill a jar with nails and broken glass; bury it under
the porch to protect a house from malicious spirits.

---

5 Sunday

2nd ♊
Color: Yellow

February

6 Monday
2nd ♊
♃ ℞ 1:52 am
☽ v/c 5:53 pm
Color: Silver

7 Tuesday
2nd ♊
☽ enters ♋ 2:03 am
☿ enters ≈ 4:35 am
Color: Red

A broom sweeps negativity away from the altar.

8 Wednesday
2nd ♋
☽ v/c 5:00 pm
Color: Topaz

Eucalyptus trees produce a powerful healing energy.

9 Thursday
2nd ♋
☽ enters ♌ 4:41 am
Color: Green

Friday
2nd ♌
Full Moon 7:33 pm
Color: Purple

Quickening Moon
Lunar eclipse 7:44 pm, 22° ♌ 28'

Set in Eastern Standard Time (EST)

Solmōnaþ (Mud Month)

The second month in the Old English calendar is *Solmōnaþ*. Anglo-Saxon scribes were familiar with the Latin word *sol* (Sun), but here the meaning comes from the Old English word *sol*, which means "mud" or "mire." Saint Bede recorded that the Anglo-Saxons gave offerings to their gods at this time by placing cakes (likely more akin to loaves of bread than sugary confections) in the first plowed furrows.

Solmōnaþ marked the end of the Yuletide. Because of this, Anglo-Saxons converting to Christianity held to a tradition observing Candlemas (February 2) as the end of the Christmas season. Candles were blessed at the church and then brought home to protect them from demons and illness.

Make all of the candles that you plan to use throughout the year in your rituals and spells. By making your own candles, you control the color and scent, and can even add a pinch of herbs or similar magical ingredients to the molten wax. If you have never made your own candles, simple kits are available at most craft stores. Solmōnaþ is a time of preparation, so create a list of your magical goals for the year.

—Alaric Albertsson

---

11 Saturday

3rd ♌
☽ v/c 12:52 am
☽ enters ♍ 8:52 am
Color: Blue

Grapefruit oil is uplifting. It relates to Saturn and earth, with masculine energy.

---

12 Sunday

3rd ♍
Color: Gold

February

13 Monday
3rd ♍
☽ v/c 7:36 am
☽ enters ♎ 3:43 pm
Color: Lavender

14 Tuesday
3rd ♎
Color: Gray

Valentine's Day

15 Wednesday
3rd ♎
☽ v/c 8:54 pm
Color: Yellow

16 Thursday
3rd ♎
☽ enters ♏ 1:41 am
Color: Turquoise

Giii is the Mayan Sun-faced fire god. He likes the number four and has control over droughts.

17 Friday
3rd ♏
☽ v/c 2:38 pm
Color: Pink

Orris root is feminine, correlating with Venus and water. It helps you to find and hold love.

☽ Saturday

3rd ♏

☉ enters ♓ 6:31 am
☽ enters ♐ 1:52 pm
4th quarter 2:33 pm
Color: Black

Sun enters Pisces
Celtic Tree Month of Ash begins

19 Sunday

4th ♐
Color: Amber

February

20 Monday
4th ♐
☽ v/c 6:37 pm
Color: Ivory

Presidents' Day

21 Tuesday
4th ♐
☽ enters ♑ 2:08 am
Color: Maroon

Rose is feminine, linked to Venus and water.
This incense enhances positive emotions.

22 Wednesday
4th ♑
☽ v/c 10:24 pm
Color: White

23 Thursday
4th ♑
☽ enters ♒ 12:17 pm
Color: Purple

Dogwood connects with the Moon and Pluto, along with
the sign of Pisces. Its leaves keep writings or meetings secret.

24 Friday
4th ♒
Color: Coral

Set in Eastern Standard Time (EST)

Amazonite

The mineral amazonite, part of the feldspar group, typically has a soft green to greenish-blue color (the green is due to lead) with bands of white or gray. It often displays an iridescent refraction of light called schiller, giving the stone a pearl-like luster, which adds to its visual appeal. It's fairly soft compared to other stones and is easily scratched. Amazonite can also fade if exposed to extreme heat or light, so handle this stone with care.

A particularly soothing stone, amazonite can be used to aid self-expression; to increase hope, courage, and confidence; and to promote universal love. Because of its association with the element of earth, it has receptive, nurturing qualities. It corresponds to the planet Uranus and has a triclinic structure. It calms nerves and is especially effective when used on the heart chakra. For any situation where you need to act with confidence and self-assurance yet also communicate with kindness, charge this stone.

I am certain, I am sure; in my actions I'm secure.
I am hopeful, I am kind: heart and mind shall be aligned.

—Ember Grant

---

25 Saturday

4th ≈
☽ v/c 1:11 pm
☿ enters ♓ 6:07 pm
☽ enters ♓ 7:24 pm
Color: Indigo

☽ Sunday

4th ♓
New Moon 9:58 am
Color: Orange

Solar eclipse 9:54 am, 8° ♓ 12'

February/March

27 Monday
1st ♓
☽ v/c 6:08 pm
☽ enters ♈ 11:52 pm
Color: White

28 Tuesday
1st ♈
Color: Black

Mardi Gras (Fat Tuesday)

1 Wednesday
1st ♈
☽ v/c 9:18 pm
Color: Topaz

Ash Wednesday

2 Thursday
1st ♈
☽ enters ♉ 2:43 am
Color: Green

3 Friday
1st ♉
☽ v/c 10:20 am
Color: Pink

*Mugwort has feminine energy, related to Venus and
earth. Use the oil to consecrate tools of divination.*

Set in Eastern Standard Time (EST)

Hrēþmōnaþ (Fierce Month)

The Anglo-Saxon people celebrated the third month of the year as *Hrēþmōnaþ*, or "Hrethe's Month." As an adjective, *hrēthe* means "fierce," which aptly describes Mother Nature's temperament at this time of year. Hrethe is an earth goddess whose name may be a variant of the continental Germanic goddess Hertha, known to the Suebi as Nerthus. Hrethe's name is also similar to the Old English *hriþer*, meaning an ox or heifer, recalling the heifers that carried the image of the continental earth mother on her annual procession, according to Tacitus.

Hrēþmōnaþ is a good time to reconnect with the earth. Get outside and do some yard work. Start a compost pile to transform a winter's accumulation of leaves and other natural debris into fertile humus. If you do not have a yard of your own, go out to a local park and clean up any trash you find there. Observe the trees growing in your vicinity. If you do not know what species they are, get a tree identification book and find out! Set out a birdbath and put a sloped rock in the center so bees and other insects can also drink without drowning. The nature spirits will thank you.

—Alaric Albertsson

---

4 Saturday

1st ♉
♀ ℞ 4:09 am
☽ enters ♊ 5:05 am
Color: Gray

Venus retrograde until April 15

○ Sunday

1st ♊
2nd quarter 6:32 am
Color: Gold

Rheda (Hrethe) is the Anglo-Saxon goddess of victory,
but she can be fickle: worship her with caution.

March

6 Monday

2nd ♊
☽ v/c 3:22 am
☽ enters ♋ 7:54 am
Color: Lavender

*The athame, traditionally a knife with a
black hilt, channels god energy to cut.*

7 Tuesday

2nd ♋
⚷ D 4:32 am
Color: Scarlet

*Chasca is a crepuscular goddess of
the Incan people, protecting virgins.*

8 Wednesday

2nd ♋
☽ v/c 9:59 am
☽ enters ♌ 11:45 am
Color: White

9 Thursday

2nd ♌
♂ enters ♉ 7:34 pm
Color: Purple

Fir stands for youth and vitality. Use it to attract prosperity.

10 Friday

2nd ♌
☽ v/c 12:06 pm
☽ enters ♍ 5:07 pm
Color: Rose

Set in Eastern Standard Time (EST)

Inside-Out Breakfast Burrito

2 large eggs (beaten)
1 burrito-sized tortilla
3 T. salsa
¾ cup precooked breakfast sausage
¾ cup sharp cheddar

Filling Variations
Sausage, sauerkraut, spicy mustard
Chorizo, jalapeño, pepper jack cheese
Chicken, pesto, and mozzarella
Corned beef, sauerkraut, Russian dressing

Spring has arrived and Ostara's blessings can be seen everywhere. The buds are beginning to swell on the trees, perennials are beginning to poke through the warming earth, and the Sun is beginning its upward climb. Since eggs are a prominent feature of this holiday, try this take on a breakfast burrito.

In a large nonstick skillet over medium-low heat, pour eggs and distribute evenly. Place tortilla on top. On one half of your tortilla, layer salsa, sausage, and cheese. Pull pan slightly off burner, cooking the half of the burrito that is clear of ingredients until eggs are cooked (3 to 5 minutes). Flip the cooked side over the filling (like a taco) and continue cooking until eggs are done and filling has heated through.

—Monica Crosson

---

11 Saturday
2nd ♍
Color: Black

☺ Sunday
2nd ♍
Full Moon 10:54 am
☽ v/c 10:36 pm
Color: Amber

Purim
Storm Moon
Daylight Saving Time begins at 2 am

March

13 Monday
3rd ♍︎
☽ enters ♎︎ 1:28 am
☿ enters ♈︎ 5:07 pm
Color: Silver

14 Tuesday
3rd ♎︎
Color: Maroon

*Thyme is feminine, belonging to Venus and water. It is a potent
antibiotic and antiviral oil popular in herbal mouthwash.*

15 Wednesday

3rd ♎︎
☽ v/c 6:05 am
☽ enters ♏︎ 11:11 am
Color: Brown

16 Thursday

3rd ♏︎
Color: Crimson

*Mother-of-pearl is pale with iridescent colors; when made into
boxes, this water material provides concealment and secrecy.*

17 Friday

3rd ♏︎
☽ v/c 5:56 pm
☽ enters ♐︎ 11:00 pm
Color: Purple

St. Patrick's Day

Set in Eastern Daylight Time (EDT)

18 Saturday
3rd ✗
Color: Indigo

Celtic Tree Month of Alder begins

19 Sunday
3rd ✗
Color: Yellow

March

☽ Monday

3rd ♐
☉ enters ♈ 6:29 am
☽ v/c 6:37 am
☽ enters ♑ 11:31 am
4th quarter 11:58 am
Color: White

Ostara/Spring Equinox
Sun enters Aries
International Astrology Day

21 Tuesday

4th ♑
Color: Black

22 Wednesday

4th ♑
☽ v/c 9:20 am
☽ enters ♒ 10:28 pm
Color: Topaz

Mint is feminine, bonded with air and Venus.
As an incense it cools and refreshes.

23 Thursday

4th ♒
Color: Green

Mahina is the Hawaiian Moon goddess, who goes
on sabbatical when her family gets on her nerves.

24 Friday

4th ♒
Color: Coral

Set in Eastern Daylight Time (EDT)

Ostara

Ostara, the vernal equinox, is the first day of spring. Many modern religious and secular traditions, including the name "Easter," come from Pagan origins. Ostara is the Germanic goddess of spring. This is when Persephone returns to the earth after ruling for six months in the underworld. A time of great promise and new growth, Ostara is a time for personal change. Ostara eggs can be a great tool for this guidance. Simply mark eggs, before or after dyeing with bright spring colors, with runes or other divinatory symbols, and then hide them around your home for your friends to find. Advise the seekers to keep their minds focused on their question while engaging in a fun and challenging Ostara egg hunt (solitaries can do a similar divination by closing their eyes and drawing them like tarot cards). Note how the symbols fall together as the hunt (or drawing) progresses. You can then charge the symbols with bright spring energy by saying a simple spring goddess name chant over them (*"Eos, Eostre, Ostre, Eostar, Ostara!"*) before eating the eggs, to "plant" the energies within, blessing yourself with the energies of spring and new beginnings!

—Thuri Calafia

---

25 Saturday

4th ≈
☽ v/c 1:56 am
☽ enters ♓ 6:06 am
Color: Blue

26 Sunday

4th ♓
Color: Orange

A wise man may change his mind, but a fool never will.

☽ Monday
4th ♓
☽ v/c 6:19 am
☽ enters ♈ 10:11 am
New Moon 10:57 pm
Color: Ivory

28 Tuesday
1st ♈
Color: Gray

Balm of Gilead is feminine, associated with Venus
and water. To heal a broken heart, carry the buds.

29 Wednesday
1st ♈
☽ v/c 8:07 am
☽ enters ♉ 11:48 am
Color: Yellow

The color of the Sun, yellow brings happiness
and optimism. Brighten your day with it.

30 Thursday
1st ♉
♀ enters ♈ 12:47 am
☽ v/c 7:12 pm
Color: Turquoise

31 Friday
1st ♉
☽ enters ♊ 12:40 pm
☿ enters ♉ 1:31 pm
Color: White

In 1972, Iceland formally recognized Asatru as a religion.

Milky Quartz

Milky quartz is the opaque, white variety of quartz. Its appearance is the result of fluids present during crystal growth, and in no way is it inferior to clear quartz. Even though it's commonly found as tumbled pieces, you can find milky quartz crystal points.

Quartz's trigonal structure combines balance with power. Yet, fluids (water element) helped it form, which adds a nurturing touch. Rather than viewing this quartz as "cloudy," think of white as clean, fresh, and new. It represents pure potential: a clean slate.

An excellent stone for personal exploration, use milky quartz to meditate on your hopes and dreams, to truly know yourself—it can remove masks and reveal your true desires. Some believe that cloudy quartz suggests hiding, but white is the opposite—it reflects. Meditate with the stone and chant this:

I am a forest—show me the trees.
I am each drop of water that makes up the sea.
Fresh as new snow on a mountain of stone,
Show me myself; reveal the unknown.

—Ember Grant

---

1 Saturday

1st ♊
Color: Black

All Fools' Day
April Fools' Day

---

2 Sunday

1st ♊
☽ v/c 10:43 am
☽ enters ♋ 2:27 pm
♀ enters ♓ 8:25 pm
Color: Yellow

April

◐ Monday

1st ♋
2nd quarter 2:39 pm
Color: Silver

4 Tuesday

2nd ♋
☽ v/c 4:45 pm
☽ enters ♌ 6:13 pm
Color: Red

*Coniraya is an Incan god of fertility and fecundity, bringing
life to everything he touches—without requiring a mate!*

5 Wednesday

2nd ♌
Color: Brown

*Brown is an earth color, associated with things that are natural
or organic. Natural wooden furniture creates a woodsy mood.*

6 Thursday

2nd ♌
♄ ℞ 1:06 am
☽ v/c 8:16 pm
Color: Crimson

*Cedar is masculine, corresponding to the Sun and fire.
Its smoke purifies space and drives away nightmares.*

7 Friday

2nd ♌
☽ enters ♍ 12:20 am
Color: Purple

Set in Eastern Daylight Time (EDT)

8 Saturday

2nd ♍
Color: Gray

9 Sunday

2nd ♍
☽ v/c 4:21 am
☽ enters ♎ 8:34 am
☿ ℞ 7:14 pm
Color: Gold

Palm Sunday
Mercury retrograde until May 3

April

10 Monday
2nd ♎︎
Color: White

☺ Tuesday
2nd ♎︎
Full Moon 2:08 am
☽ v/c 2:19 pm
☽ enters ♏︎ 6:42 pm
Color: Black

Wind Moon
Passover begins

12 Wednesday
3rd ♏︎
Color: Topaz

*Iceland spar is a clear refractive stone whose air
influence can double the power of any charm bag.*

13 Thursday
3rd ♏︎
Color: Turquoise

14 Friday
3rd ♏︎
☽ v/c 12:18 am
☽ enters ♐︎ 6:27 am
Color: Coral

Good Friday
Orthodox Good Friday

Set in Eastern Daylight Time (EDT)

Ēostremōnaþ (A Feast for Eostre)

Ēostremōnaþ is "Eostre's Month," the time to celebrate the feast of the goddess Eostre. Eostre is the English name of the Germanic goddess Ostara. Her feast coincidentally took place near the Christians' Paschal feast, and her name was retained for the latter in both Modern English (Easter) and German (Ostern). Eostre is a goddess of spring and the dawn—a goddess of new beginnings. Her name is related to "east," where the Sun rises.

Many traditional Easter visuals—rabbits, eggs, chicks, and ducks—are celebrations of the fertility and renewal of spring. Eggs are one of the most persistent Easter traditions, because of both their representation of renewed life and their abundance. In a natural environment, hens lay more eggs in the spring than any other season. Have your friends over for an egg-dyeing party, with a prize for the most creative egg! The eggs can be decorated with runes or other Pagan symbols, or anything your imagination conjures up.

Give your home a thorough spring cleaning. As a goddess of new beginnings, Eostre exalts us to clear away the old and make way for new opportunities and possibilities.

—Alaric Albertsson

---

15 Saturday

3rd ♐
♀ D 6:18 am
Color: Indigo

Celtic Tree Month of Willow begins

---

16 Sunday

3rd ♐
☽ v/c 2:26 pm
☽ enters ♑ 7:05 pm
Color: Amber

Easter
Orthodox Easter

April

17 Monday

3rd ♑
Color: Lavender

18 Tuesday

3rd ♑
Color: Scarlet

Passover ends

☽ Wednesday

3rd ♑
☽ v/c 5:57 am
4th quarter 5:57 am
☽ enters ♒ 6:52 am
☉ enters ♉ 5:27 pm
Color: White

Sun enters Taurus

20 Thursday

4th ♒
♇ ℞ 8:49 am
☿ enters ♈ 1:37 pm
Color: Purple

21 Friday

4th ♒
♂ enters ♊ 6:32 am
☽ v/c 2:23 pm
☽ enters ♓ 3:43 pm
Color: Pink

Willow trees, which grow near water,
aid lunar magic and processing grief.

Chocolate Love Bars

1 box chocolate fudge or
   devil's food cake mix
2 eggs
⅓ cup vegetable oil
2 8 oz. packages cream cheese
⅓ cup sugar
6 oz. sour cream
1 can black cherry pie filling (optional)
Whipped cream (optional)

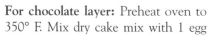

For chocolate layer: Preheat oven to 350° F. Mix dry cake mix with 1 egg and oil until crumbly and coarse. Reserve 1 cup of crumbs for topping. Pat remaining crumbs into a 13 × 9 × 2-inch baking dish. Bake for 15 minutes.

   For cheesecake layer: Beat cream cheese, sugar, egg, and sour cream until smooth and light. Spread over chocolate layer and sprinkle remaining crumbs on top. Bake an additional 15 minutes. Let cool in refrigerator for approximately 1 hour. Cut into bars and serve with a dollop of cherry pie filling and whipped cream (optional, but don't skimp if you do).

   Beltane deserves a dessert to match its lusty reputation. This one is rich, decadent, and easy to prepare. Lay out a blanket under May's passionate sky and enjoy this one with your consort!

—Monica Crosson

22 Saturday

4th ♓
Color: Brown

Earth Day

23 Sunday

4th ♓
☽ v/c 5:34 pm
☽ enters ♈ 8:32 pm
Color: Gold

April

24 Monday
4th ♈
Color: Ivory

A feather or a fan is used to spread smoke from incense or other sources. It corresponds to air.

25 Tuesday
4th ♈
☽ v/c 5:53 pm
☽ enters ♉ 9:56 pm
Color: Gray

☽ Wednesday
4th ♉
New Moon 8:16 am
Color: Yellow

Dyaus is an Indian sky god who once divided himself in half.

27 Thursday
1st ♉
☽ v/c 9:18 pm
☽ enters ♊ 9:39 pm
Color: Green

The altar cloth protects the altar and may also match correspondences for the working. Ideally it should be washable.

28 Friday
1st ♊
♀ enters ♈ 9:13 am
Color: Rose

Set in Eastern Daylight Time (EDT)

Howlite

Howlite does not have a long meta-physical history, but its popularity is increasing due to its affordability and availability. It's an opaque, white stone with veins of gray or black that can produce decorative designs, making it ideal for beads and cabochon jewelry. However, because of its abundance, it can be dyed to create false turquoise. In addition, sometimes howlite is sold as white buffalo stone, which is actually a different stone and quite rare.

Howlite has a monoclinic structure, giving it qualities of stability, clarity, and encouragement. It promotes ambition with patience, can increase the desire for knowledge, and improves communication—especially in tense situations. It's an ideal stone for those moments when you need careful communication skills.

Use this chant to charge the stone, and carry it with you or place it in the appropriate location of an important meeting:

Knowing what to say and when: / The best way to begin and end.
When to listen, when to speak; / I always know the right technique.

—Ember Grant

---

29 Saturday
1st ♊
♃ enters ♊ 11:42 am
☽ v/c 5:28 pm
☽ enters ♋ 9:48 pm
Color: Blue

---

30 Sunday
1st ♋
Color: Orange

A reputation, like fine china, is easily cracked and poorly mended.

May

1 Monday
1st ♋
☽ v/c 4:23 pm
Color: Gray

Beltane/May Day

☽ Tuesday
1st ♋
☽ enters ♌ 12:12 am
♥ enters ♌ 7:57 pm
2nd quarter 10:47 pm
Color: Maroon

3 Wednesday
2nd ♌
☿ D 12:33 pm
Color: Topaz

Cypress is the best wood for a Maypole.

4 Thursday
2nd ♌
☽ v/c 12:35 am
☽ enters ♍ 5:47 am
Color: Turquoise

5 Friday
2nd ♍
Color: Rose

Cinco de Mayo
Beltane crossquarter day
(Sun reaches 15° Taurus)

Set in Eastern Daylight Time (EDT)

Beltane

Beltane, or May Eve, is the day before May Day, a traditional day for dancing around a Maypole. In ancient times, couples would go out on Beltane to gather flowers for the next day's festivities, often making love under the starry sky in the process. The next morning, they would bring the flowers back to the village, which was referred to as "bringing in the May."

Today, most Pagan Beltane traditions include dancing around a Maypole, drinking May wine, and, often, choosing and blessing a May King and May Queen. May wine is easy to make and delicious. Simply take a handful of sweet woodruff, rinse well, and toss into a large punch bowl. Add sliced lemons or strawberries and cover with white wine (sparkling wines are even more festive). Let the brew stand for thirty minutes to one hour and serve.

If you don't have room for a traditional Maypole, you could try making some May gads. These are simply sticks that have been gathered from nature ahead of time, to which one attaches and weaves, Maypole-style, brightly colored ribbons. Then, the May gads can be "planted" in the garden or even in plant pots to bless and brighten one's personal space.

—Thuri Calafia

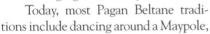

6 Saturday

2nd ♍
☽ v/c 8:42 am
☽ enters ♎ 2:20 pm
Color: Indigo

Opal's brilliant colors relate to fire, helping to manifest grand ideas in the physical realm.

7 Sunday

2nd ♎
Color: Amber

May

8 Monday
2nd ♎︎
☽ v/c 6:59 pm
Color: Silver

Honeysuckle oil has masculine associations, belonging to Jupiter
and earth. Rub on the forehead to enhance spiritual vision.

9 Tuesday
2nd ♎︎
☽ enters ♏︎ 1:01 am
☿ ℞ 7:06 pm
Color: Red

☺ Wednesday
2nd ♏︎
☽ v/c 5:42 pm
Full Moon 5:42 pm
Color: Yellow

Flower Moon

11 Thursday
3rd ♏︎
☽ enters ♐︎ 12:59 pm
Color: Purple

12 Friday
3rd ♐︎
Color: Pink

A cricket in the house brings good luck.

13 Saturday

3rd ♐

☽ v/c 10:14 pm

Color: Blue

Celtic Tree Month of Hawthorn begins

14 Sunday

3rd ♐

☽ enters ♑ 1:37 am

Color: Orange

Mother's Day

May

15 Monday
3rd ♑
Color: Ivory

Vervain is feminine, in correspondence with Venus and earth. Place under the pillow for dreams and inspiration.

16 Tuesday
3rd ♑
☿ enters ♉ 12:07 am
☽ v/c 6:22 am
☽ enters ♒ 1:50 pm
Color: Black

17 Wednesday
3rd ♒
Color: White

The earliest human altars date from around 75,000 BCE and show signs of worship of animals including bears and wolves.

○ Thursday
3rd ♒
☽ v/c 8:33 pm
4th quarter 8:33 pm
☽ enters ♓ 11:52 pm
Color: Crimson

19 Friday
4th ♓
Color: Coral

Goldstone is usually brown but has a blue form too, both related to fire. Use it to boost human ingenuity.

Þrimilci (The Three Milkings)

The beginning of summer is ushered in with the *Þrimilci* Moon. Saint Bede's writing tells us this is the month when the Anglo-Saxon people milked their cows three times a day. Cattle were bred in the summer to ensure forage would be available when calves were dropped the next spring, as fodder was precious and they relied more on natural forage. The flush of fresh, green herbage nourished not only the calves but also their mothers. By Þrimilci, the calves were weaned and the milk of the cows was in full flow.

Þrimilci is all about abundance, in particular the abundant bounty of the earth. Tap into the magic of the season by planting an herb garden. Traditional Anglo-Saxon herbs include mugwort, betony, comfrey, elecampane, fennel, horehound, parsley, rosemary, and vervain, but be sure to choose herbs that you have some culinary or magical use for. If you cannot plant an outside garden, perhaps you can grow a few herbs in a windowsill with good exposure to the Sun. Chives, basil, thyme, sage, and rosemary are a few herbs that can be successfully grown indoors.

—Alaric Albertsson

---

20 Saturday

4th ♓
☉ enters ♊ 4:31 pm
☽ v/c 11:39 pm
Color: Gray

Sun enters Gemini

---

21 Sunday

4th ♓
☽ enters ♈ 6:10 am
Color: Yellow

May

22 Monday
4th ♈
Color: Lavender

Haokah is the Sioux god of thunder, a trickster who cries when happy and laughs when sad.

23 Tuesday
4th ♈
☽ v/c 2:59 am
☽ enters ♉ 8:33 am
Color: Scarlet

The chalice, a goblet often made of silver, channels goddess energy to cleanse.

24 Wednesday
4th ♉
☽ v/c 3:08 pm
Color: Brown

☽ Thursday
4th ♉
☽ enters ♊ 8:15 am
New Moon 3:44 pm
Color: Green

26 Friday
1st ♊
Color: Purple

England repealed the last of its anti-Witchcraft laws in 1951.

Set in Eastern Daylight Time (EDT)

Lodestone

The mineral lodestone is a natural magnet. It's magnetite, an iron oxide mineral. There is some mystery as to how pieces of this mineral become magnetized—not all pieces are. A true lodestone will actually attract tiny iron filings.

Lodestone has a cubic structure and is associated with the planet Venus and the element of water. It combines stability with receptivity; it's firm but gentle. Use it like a compass to keep yourself on course—personally, professionally, or both. Its other properties include motivation, guidance, and direction. It can aid balancing, recognizing duality, and can be used to promote fidelity. Keep lodestone dry: charge it in sunlight, but don't cleanse it with water. Instead, place it on a bed of salt.

To use lodestone for helping you stay focused on a goal, visualize and use this chant. Carry the stone with you, or keep it somewhere you can see it every day.

Keep me going, stay on track. / Don't hesitate—no looking back.
I don't need to reach perfection; / Just point me in the right direction.

—Ember Grant

---

27 Saturday

1st ♊
☽ v/c 2:18 am
☽ enters ♋ 7:25 am
Color: Black

Ramadan begins

---

28 Sunday

1st ♋
Color: Gold

May/June

29 Monday
1st ♋
☽ v/c 2:59 am
☽ enters ♌ 8:12 am
Color: Silver

Memorial Day

30 Tuesday
1st ♌
Color: White

31 Wednesday
1st ♌
☽ v/c 7:14 am
☽ enters ♍ 12:16 pm
Color: Topaz

Shavuot

◐ Thursday
1st ♍
2nd quarter 8:42 am
Color: Purple

2 Friday
2nd ♍
☽ v/c 5:48 pm
☽ enters ♎ 8:04 pm
Color: Pink

Pink is innovative and feminine, a lovely choice for craft rooms or goddess shrines.

3 Saturday

2nd ♎
Color: Indigo

Ba-ja is a Chinese god of scarecrows, with an eagle's beak and talons, blue skin, and a general's cloak.

4 Sunday

2nd ♎
♂ enters ♋ 12:16 pm
Color: Orange

5 Monday
2nd ♎
☽ v/c 4:57 am
☽ enters ♏ 6:46 am
Color: Ivory

6 Tuesday
2nd ♏
♀ enters ♉ 3:27 am
☿ enters ♊ 6:15 pm
☽ v/c 8:35 pm
Color: Scarlet

*If you catch a falling leaf before it touches
the ground, you may make a wish.*

7 Wednesday
2nd ♏
☽ enters ♐ 6:59 pm
Color: Brown

*Pink-and-green unakite blends the energies of Mars and Venus,
male and female, making it great for relationship work.*

8 Thursday
2nd ♐
Color: White

☺ Friday
2nd ♐
Full Moon 9:10 am
♃ D 10:03 am
Color: Rose

Strong Sun Moon

Ærre Līþa (Early Litha)

Anglo-Saxons knew June as Early Litha (*Ærre Līþa*). The Summer Solstice is one of the most important events on the Old English calendar, second only to Yule. *Līþa* means "gentle," and in this context refers to the two months notable in Britain for their relatively mild temperatures, June and July. Just like the Yuletide season, the Old English year celebrates a two-month Litha season. At this time Sunne, the Sun goddess, comes into her full glory.

Since there are more than twelve lunar cycles in a solar year, the Old English calendar periodically added an extra month between Ærre Līþa and Æfterra Līþa known simply as Līþa. Years with thirteen months were called *þrilīþa* (Three Lithas) years. The solstice, or Midsummer, was traditionally celebrated with bonfires and divinations. Midsummer's Eve was especially efficacious for love divinations. If you are seeking love, pick a sprig of St. John's wort on Midsummer's Eve and place it under your pillow or somewhere close as you sleep. Tradition has it that the herb's freshness the following morning indicates your prospects of finding your true love during the coming year.

—Alaric Albertsson

---

10 Saturday

3rd ♐
☽ v/c 2:20 am
☽ enters ♑ 7:36 am
Color: Black

Celtic Tree Month of Oak begins

---

11 Sunday

3rd ♑
Color: Gold

June

12 Monday
3rd ♑
☽ v/c 2:45 pm
☽ enters ♒ 7:45 pm
Color: White

*Mulberry trees often grow in hedgerows; they
stand for knowledge, wisdom, and willpower.*

13 Tuesday
3rd ♒
Color: Red

14 Wednesday
3rd ♒
Color: Yellow

Flag Day

15 Thursday
3rd ♒
☽ v/c 1:40 am
☽ enters ♓ 6:17 am
Color: Turquoise

16 Friday
3rd ♓
♆ ℞ 7:09 am
Color: Coral

Set in Eastern Daylight Time (EDT)

Strawberry Basil Icebox Cake

4 cups heavy cream
3 T. sugar
1 T. vanilla
1 14 oz. box of graham crackers, crushed
4 cups sliced strawberries
1 cup basil leaves, chopped
Strawberries and basil for garnish

Whip heavy cream, sugar, and vanilla until stiff. In a 13 × 9 × 2-inch baking dish, spread a thin layer of the whipped cream. Follow this with a layer of graham crackers. Add a thicker layer of whipped cream followed by a layer of strawberries, and then sprinkle some of your chopped basil. Repeat this process until you have come to the top of the dish. Finally cap it off with a final layer of whipped cream. Cover in plastic wrap and leave in your refrigerator overnight. Before serving, slice up a few more berries and add them to the top. Serve each slice with a basil leaf garnish.

The Full Moon around Midsummer was known as the Strawberry Moon to the Algonquin peoples of North America. A summertime favorite, the strawberry is especially tasty as an added ingredient in old-fashioned icebox cake. Make it the day before your festivities, and enjoy its cool deliciousness with friends.

—Monica Crosson

☽ Saturday

3rd ♓
☽ v/c 7:33 am
4th quarter 7:33 am
☽ enters ♈ 1:55 pm
Color: Gray

Pine is masculine, related to fire and Mars;
burn it for grounding and strength.

---

18 Sunday

4th ♈
Color: Orange

Father's Day

---

19 Monday
4th ♈︎
☽ v/c 3:42 pm
☽ enters ♉︎ 5:53 pm
Color: Silver

20 Tuesday
4th ♉︎
Color: Maroon

*Chili pepper is masculine, linked with Mars
and fire. Sprinkle the powder to break hexes.*

21 Wednesday
4th ♉︎
☉ enters ♋︎ 12:24 am
☽ v/c 12:26 am
☿ enters ♋︎ 5:57 am
☽ enters ♊︎ 6:44 pm
Color: Topaz

Sun enters Cancer
Midsummer/Litha/Summer Solstice

22 Thursday
4th ♊︎
Color: Green

☽ Friday
4th ♊︎
☽ v/c 2:45 pm
☽ enters ♋︎ 6:07 pm
New Moon 10:31 pm
Color: Purple

Litha

Litha, the Summer Solstice, is the time when the Earth, in her elliptical path around the Sun, slows down before making her journey around the other side. The word *solstice* means "Sun standstill," because the ancients thought it was the Sun, not the Earth, that seemed to stand still. The full solstice event lasts about three days.

This is a good time to take stock and assess the growth of one's garden, both the inner garden as well as the outer, physical one. Although the harvest festivals are a ways off, Litha is still a time to focus on abundance and appreciate summer's bounty. This is also when the Holly King, the Dark God of the dying year, conquers the Oak King, the Sun God. It can be fun and richly satisfying to reenact this mock battle in ritual, reminding us of the need for both the light and the dark, for even as the Dark God reigns, temperatures continue to rise, and crops keep growing and ripening, giving their life force so that we may keep on living.

Litha is a magical time for wishing. One tradition is to hold a rose, thinking of what you wish to bring into your life, and then release it onto a body of water, thereby releasing your wish to the Goddess.

—Thuri Calafia

---

24 Saturday

1st ♋
Color: Blue

Päivätär is the Finnish goddess of summer, associated with the Sun and eggs.

---

25 Sunday

1st ♋
☽ v/c 2:44 pm
☽ enters ♌ 6:06 pm
Color: Amber

Ramadan ends

---

26 Monday

1st ♌

♀ enters ♉ 10:34 pm

Color: Lavender

Around 2000 BCE, The Epic of Gilgamesh, in which Enkidu gives hints of magical or werewolf-like qualities, emerged.

27 Tuesday

1st ♌

☽ v/c 5:12 pm

☽ enters ♍ 8:41 pm

Color: Gray

28 Wednesday

1st ♍

Color: White

Pellervoinen is the Finnish god of agriculture, who wakes in spring to dance around sowing crops.

29 Thursday

1st ♍

☽ v/c 4:35 pm

Color: Crimson

○ Friday

1st ♍

☽ enters ♎ 3:02 am

2nd quarter 8:51 pm

Color: Coral

Ametrine

Ametrine is a blend of amethyst and citrine, resulting in a crystal that combines qualities of both minerals and has a striking pale violet and yellow appearance. This union is reportedly caused by temperature changes during the crystal's formation due to oxidation of iron in the stone. This dynamic duo can be used to release blockages and negativity, transforming it into something constructive. Ametrine also promotes insight, creativity, and compatibility, and can help you reach higher states of attunement during meditation. Charge it in sunlight but briefly, as the color can fade.

Use ametrine to rise above setbacks or to confront negative thought patterns that are holding you back. Hold the stone and gaze upon it, visualizing yourself being light and free from worry. Carry the stone with you, ideally against your skin. Repeat this meditation to lift your spirits:

I am light—I release what pulls me down.
I am light—to no sorrow am I bound.
I am light—I will turn it all around.

—Ember Grant

---

1 Saturday

2nd ♎
☿ ℞ 3:09 am
Color: Brown

Keep an acorn in the attic to deter lightning.

---

2 Sunday

2nd ♎
☽ v/c 9:16 am
☽ enters ♏ 12:59 pm
Color: Gold

July

3 Monday

2nd ♏
Color: Gray

4 Tuesday

2nd ♏
♀ enters ♊ 8:11 pm
☽ v/c 9:34 pm
Color: White

Independence Day

5 Wednesday
2nd ♏
☽ enters ♐ 1:08 am
☿ enters ♌ 8:20 pm
Color: Topaz

6 Thursday
2nd ♐
Color: Turquoise

Larimar is a blue water stone used for healing baths;
it cleanses the body of infections or old traumas.

7 Friday
2nd ♐
☽ v/c 10:12 am
☽ enters ♑ 1:45 pm
Color: Purple

8 Saturday

2nd ♑
Color: Blue

Celtic Tree Month of Holly begins

☺ Sunday

2nd ♑
Full Moon 12:07 am
☽ v/c 10:12 pm
Color: Yellow

Blessing Moon

July

10 Monday
3rd ♑
☽ enters ♒ 1:35 am
♀ enters ♋ 7:47 am
Color: Ivory

11 Tuesday
3rd ♒
Color: Red

*The thorns of holly ward off evil and
symbolize the dark half of the year.*

12 Wednesday
3rd ♒
☽ v/c 8:40 am
☽ enters ♓ 11:51 am
Color: Brown

13 Thursday
3rd ♓
Color: Green

*Dill yields a sweet oil for compassion and tenderness, ideal
for fathers. It is masculine, relating to Mercury and fire.*

14 Friday
3rd ♓
☽ v/c 1:00 pm
☽ enters ♈ 7:52 pm
Color: White

*Elat is a Middle Eastern mother goddess
who bore seventy-seven gods.*

Æfterra Līþa (Late Litha)

Just as the Winter Solstice is followed in the Old English calendar by the month of Late Yule, the Summer Solstice is followed by Late Litha. In the wake of Midsummer, Sunne begins to wane and the days become shorter. Flax can now be harvested and hay cut and stored for winter fodder.

Although most grains are harvested in the late summer and autumn, under ideal conditions winter wheat can be harvested as early as July. This early grain had to be dried, winnowed, threshed, and ground to become useful as flour by Lammas (the "loaf mass"), which celebrated the bread baked from the early harvest. In the Christian era, the first loaves were brought to the church to be blessed. The blessed loaves were then sometimes used to work magic, protecting the rest of the harvested grain. In the ninth-century *Anglo-Saxon Chronicle*, Lammas is called the "feast of first fruits."

Bake bread and hold your own harvest celebration. Either make the bread from scratch or, if you prefer, purchase ready-to-bake dough found in the freezer section at the supermarket. After your loaf has risen, invite your friends over so everyone can enjoy the heady aroma of the baking bread.

—Alaric Albertsson

---

15 Saturday
3rd ♈
Color: Black

◖ Sunday
3rd ♈
4th quarter 3:26 pm
☽ v/c 10:19 pm
Color: Orange

An incense burner holds fragrant resins as they burn, evoking fire.

July

17 Monday

4th ♈︎
☽ enters ♉︎ 1:04 am
⚸ enters ♍︎ 7:15 pm
Color: Lavender

18 Tuesday

4th ♉︎
Color: Scarlet

*Agrimony is masculine, corresponding to air and Jupiter.
Stuffed in a dream pillow, it brings protection and sleep.*

19 Wednesday

4th ♉︎
☽ v/c 2:11 am
☽ enters ♊︎ 3:31 am
Color: White

*Vajravarathi is a Tibetan animal goddess;
she is entirely red and has the face of a sow.*

20 Thursday

4th ♊︎
♂ enters ♌︎ 8:19 am
Color: Crimson

*Gum arabic is masculine, relating to the Sun
and the air. Burn it to access psychic powers.*

21 Friday

4th ♊︎
☽ v/c 1:41 am
☽ enters ♋︎ 4:09 am
Color: Rose

Set in Eastern Daylight Time (EDT)

Kyanite

Blue like the sky, the mineral kyanite can range from deep shades of azure to pale pastel and has a fibrous, blade-like appearance. It can be other colors, but most prefer the classic sky blue.

Kyanite can help achieve tranquility, balance, attunement, and psychic awareness and increase creativity and personal expression. It aligns all the chakras but is most useful for the throat and third eye. It can help clear confusion, promote compassion, and is an excellent meditation stone. Its triclinic structure makes it quite useful in one's personal life, especially regarding perceptions and attitudes.

Perhaps you've noticed this while flying in an airplane: even when it's stormy, above the clouds all is clear, bright, and blue. Use kyanite in this affirmation to find peace in a time of stress. Let it remind you that despite what's going on around you, it will pass—and there's a peaceful place inside you. Like the sky above the clouds, it's quiet there.

Above the rain, above the clouds, / It's calm and peaceful all around.
As within, so without, / I rise above the storm of doubt.

—Ember Grant

22 Saturday

4th ♋
☉ enters ♌ 11:15 am
Color: Indigo

- Sun enters Leo

☽ Sunday

4th ♋
☽ v/c 2:05 am
☽ enters ♌ 4:34 am
New Moon 5:46 am
Color: Amber

24 Monday

1st ♌
Color: Silver

*Lavender is masculine, matching Mercury
and air. This incense attracts love.*

25 Tuesday

1st ♌
☽ v/c 5:22 am
☽ enters ♍ 6:32 am
☿ enters ♍ 7:41 pm
Color: Gray

26 Wednesday

1st ♍
Color: Yellow

*Lion statues at the base of a staircase
frighten away negative entities.*

27 Thursday

1st ♍
☽ v/c 2:31 am
☽ enters ♎ 11:37 am
Color: Purple

28 Friday

1st ♎
Color: Pink

*Earthy kornerupine comes in yellow to brown and
helps break barriers to free you from oppression.*

　　　Set in Eastern Daylight Time (EDT)

Corn Pudding

3 T. butter
6 ears fresh corn, cut off the cob
 (about 3 cups)
1 medium green pepper, chopped
1 medium onion, chopped
4 eggs
1 tsp. honey
2 cups half and half
Fresh thyme leaves (to taste)
¼ tsp. salt
⅛ tsp. pepper

Melt butter in large skillet. Add corn, peppers, and onions and sauté for 3 to 5 minutes. Remove from heat and set aside. In a large bowl, beat eggs. Stir in half and half, honey, thyme, salt, pepper, and corn mixture. Pour into buttered 1½-quart casserole dish. Stand casserole dish in a shallow pan with enough hot water to reach halfway up the side of the dish. Bake at 325° F for 50 minutes, or until a knife inserted in the center comes out clean.

The dog days of summer have arrived, and with them comes Lughnasadh. This recipe is an old-time favorite, and corn is a prevalent feature of the first of three harvest festivals. As the light begins to shift, we turn to the harvest and thank the Goddess for her abundance.

—Monica Crosson

---

29 Saturday

1st ♎
☽ v/c 5:30 pm
☽ enters ♏ 8:23 pm
Color: Gray

Gray represents practicality and moderation.
Use it to avoid extremes.

○ Sunday

1st ♏
2nd quarter 11:23 am
Color: Yellow

July/August

31 Monday
2nd ♏
☽ v/c 7:10 am
♀ enters ♋ 10:54 am
Color: White

1 Tuesday
2nd ♏
☽ enters ♐ 8:01 am
Color: Black

Lammas/Lughnasadh

2 Wednesday
2nd ♐
Color: White

Marigold is masculine, related to the Sun and fire. Use it in rituals about death or the dead.

3 Thursday
2nd ♐
♅ ℞ 1:31 am
☽ v/c 5:38 pm
☽ enters ♑ 8:37 pm
Color: Crimson

4 Friday
2nd ♑
Color: Coral

Bacchus has drowned more people than Neptune.

Set in Eastern Daylight Time (EDT)

Lughnasadh

Lughnasadh, or August Eve, is cele-brated by some on July 31 and others on August 1. Also called Lammas ("loaf mass") in the Christian tradition, Lughnasadh marks the first of the three great harvest festivals, the grain harvest. In many traditions, it commemorates the blessing of the bread. Lughnasadh is also time of sacrifice, of willingly giving up something to make room in our lives for something new. This is often a bad habit or negative

thought pattern, though in some traditions, it is a time of charity and give-aways. We can clean out our pantries and closets, incorporating a blessing of these goods into our rituals before giving them to a favorite charity. Fun and meaningful ways to celebrate Lughnasadh include making decorations with dried corn, such as an eight-spoked Sun wheel that symbolizes the eight sabbats, and the baking and sharing of bread. If you make yeast breads, sprout a handful of whole grains (wheat, oats, or barley) a few days before making your sacred loaves to symbolize the God, who died at Litha and is now growing in the womb of the Goddess. You can even shape the bread dough to look like Lugh or another Sun god and serve it for your cakes and wine in ritual.

—Thuri Calafia

5 Saturday
2nd ♑
Color: Indigo

Celtic Tree Month of Hazel begins

6 Sunday
2nd ♑
☽ v/c 5:22 am
☽ enters ♒ 8:15 am
Color: Amber

August

☺ Monday

2nd ≈

Full Moon 2:11 pm

Color: White

Corn Moon

Lunar eclipse 2:21 pm, 15° ≈ 25'

Lammas crossquarter day (Sun reaches 15° Leo)

8 Tuesday

3rd ≈

☽ v/c 3:07 pm

☽ enters ♓ 5:56 pm

Color: Gray

9 Wednesday

3rd ♓

Color: Yellow

10 Thursday

3rd ♓

☽ v/c 9:38 am

Color: Purple

*Variscite is a blue-green stone striped with brown
whose earth energy excels at finding ley lines.*

11 Friday

3rd ♓

☽ enters ♈ 1:22 am

Color: Pink

*Fennel carries masculine power, matching Mercury
and fire. Wear the oil to solve problems.*

Set in Eastern Daylight Time (EDT)

12 Saturday

3rd ♈
☿ ℞ 9:00 pm
Color: Blue

Mercury retrograde until September 5

13 Sunday

3rd ♈
☽ v/c 4:01 am
☽ enters ♉ 6:40 am
Color: Yellow

◗ Monday
3rd ♉
☽ v/c 9:15 pm
4th quarter 9:15 pm
Color: Lavender

Zosim is the Slavic god of bees, mead, and bawdy songs.

15 Tuesday
4th ♉
☽ enters ♊ 10:06 am
Color: Maroon

16 Wednesday
4th ♊
Color: Topaz

17 Thursday
4th ♊
☽ v/c 9:38 am
☽ enters ♋ 12:13 pm
Color: Turquoise

Hyacinth is masculine, relating to Mars
and water; burn this incense for happiness.

18 Friday
4th ♋
Color: Purple

Wēodmōnaþ (Weed Month)

The Weed Month (*Wēodmōnaþ*) is so named for August's fast-growing weeds. Barley, rye, and oats were traditionally harvested at this time of year, but invasive plants could ruin cabbages, leeks, turnips, and similar crops if not kept in check. This was accomplished with a "weedhook," an implement similar to a modern hoe. Then as now a weed usually implied an unwanted plant, but *wēod* could also be used to describe any wild herb.

Identify things in your life that may be choking your creativity: people, habits, unhealthy situations. Cut paper into one-inch strips and write the name of one thing that inhibits you on each strip. After you've prepared your paper strips, burn an incense of dried fern and dill weed. Hold each strip of paper in the incense, then crush the paper in your hand as you say, *"I remove this from the garden of my life."* Visualize the obstacle fading away. The crushed papers may then be either burned, composted, or buried.

Go out and gather wild herbs. Plantain, shepherd's purse, dandelion, spearmint, and red clover are among the many herbs that can be found growing in natural settings. (Do not ingest an herb unless you know it is edible.)

—Alaric Albertsson

19 Saturday

4th ♋
☽ v/c 11:17 am
☽ enters ♌ 1:55 pm
Color: Black

20 Sunday

4th ♌
Color: Gold

The pentacle, which may be marked on a tile or stone, channels Goddess energy to protect.

August

☽ Monday
4th ♌
☽ v/c 2:30 pm
New Moon 2:30 pm
☽ enters ♍ 4:25 pm
Color: Ivory

Solar eclipse 2:25 pm, 28° ♌ 53'

22 Tuesday
1st ♍
☉ enters ♍ 6:20 pm
Color: Scarlet

Sun enters Virgo

23 Wednesday
1st ♍
☽ v/c 4:02 pm
☽ enters ♎ 9:05 pm
Color: Brown

24 Thursday
1st ♎
Color: Green

*Citronella oil is masculine, corresponding to the Sun and
fire. It banishes insects and other unwanted beings.*

25 Friday
1st ♎
♄ D 8:08 am
Color: Rose

Set in Eastern Daylight Time (EDT)

Sodalite

Sodalite is typically dark blue with veins of black, white, or gray, making it a popular stone for cabochon jewelry and tumbled pieces. Its name comes from the mineral's sodium content. Sodalite has a cubic structure, making it especially good for practical purposes, yet it also has associations with inspiration and the arts—a good combination for those who need to balance creativity with rationality. It can be used with throat and brow chakras.

Sodalite promotes logic and self-esteem, eliminates confusion, and is good for times when fellowship is needed to get something done. It's perfect for use in groups to foster trust and intellectual stimulation. It can establish companionship and pave the way for calm communication.

When you need help working with others—especially when the situation calls for a blend of intellect, creativity, and order—charge sodalite and place it in the room. If possible, charge the stone when the Moon is waxing or full, ideally when the Moon is in the sign of Libra.

As a group we act as one.
Inspire, think, and get it done.

—Ember Grant

26 Saturday

1st ♎︎
♀ enters ♌︎ 12:30 am
☽ v/c 1:39 am
☽ enters ♏︎ 4:53 am
✶ D 1:14 pm
Color: Gray

○ Sunday

1st ♏︎
Color: Amber

Linden trees bear sweet flowers that make marvelous tea or honey.

28 Monday
1st ♏︎
☽ v/c 5:38 am
☽ enters ♐︎ 3:48 pm
Color: Silver

29 Tuesday
1st ♐︎
2nd quarter 4:13 am
Color: Red

Draupathi is an Indian fire goddess who walks over hot coals.

30 Wednesday
2nd ♐︎
Color: Topaz

*Heather is feminine, belonging to Venus and
water. Shake a wet bough to bring the rain.*

31 Thursday
2nd ♐︎
☽ v/c 12:42 am
☽ enters ♑︎ 4:18 am
☿ enters ♌︎ 11:28 am
Color: White

1 Friday
2nd ♑︎
Color: Purple

*Purple stands for power and wisdom,
so it is well suited to clergy or elders.*

Mabon Raw Apple Cake

Cake

2 eggs (beaten)
½ cup vegetable oil
2 cups brown sugar
1 tsp. vanilla
2 cups flour
2 tsp. baking soda
1 T. cinnamon
¼ tsp. salt
4 cups grated apples
1 cup chopped walnuts

Frosting

8 oz. cream cheese
3 T. butter
1½ cups powdered sugar
½ tsp. vanilla

Preheat oven to 350° F and grease and flour a 9 × 13-inch pan. Beat together eggs, oil, brown sugar, and vanilla. Sift flour, baking soda, cinnamon, and salt, and add it to your wet mixture. Fold in apples and walnuts and bake for 45 minutes or until a knife inserted in the middle of the cake comes out clean. For the frosting, beat together cream cheese, butter, powdered sugar, and vanilla until nice and creamy.

—Monica Crosson

---

2 Saturday

2nd ♑
☽ v/c 12:30 pm
☽ enters ♒ 4:06 pm
Color: Blue

Celtic Tree Month of Vine begins

---

3 Sunday

2nd ♒
Color: Yellow

September

4 Monday

2nd ♒
Color: Gray

Labor Day

5 Tuesday

2nd ♒
☽ v/c 1:15 am
☽ enters ♓ 1:28 am
♂ enters ♍ 5:35 am
☿ D 7:29 am
Color: Maroon

*Yucca is masculine, relating to the Moon and
water. Plant it to aid in transformation.*

☺ Wednesday

2nd ♓
Full Moon 3:03 am
☽ v/c 4:29 pm
Color: White

Harvest Moon

7 Thursday

3rd ♓
☽ enters ♈ 8:01 am
Color: Crimson

8 Friday

3rd ♈
Color: Coral

*Hawk's eye is an earth stone with shamanic properties,
suited for astral travel or other magical journeys.*

Set in Eastern Daylight Time (EDT)

9 Saturday

3rd ♈︎
☽ v/c 11:52 am
☽ enters ♉︎ 12:23 pm
☿ enters ♍︎ 10:52 pm
Color: Indigo

10 Sunday

3rd ♉︎
☽ v/c 8:54 pm
Color: Gold

If you see ants fighting, that means an enemy is near.

September

11 Monday

3rd ♉
♀ ℞ 1:46 pm
☽ enters ♊ 3:29 pm
Color: Silver

12 Tuesday

3rd ♊
Color: Red

Red draws attention and boosts excitement.
Use it to designate a focal point.

☽ Wednesday

3rd ♊
4th quarter 2:25 am
☽ v/c 2:35 pm
☽ enters ♋ 6:12 pm
Color: Brown

14 Thursday

4th ♋
Color: Green

Elyōn is the High God of the Middle East whose
attendants ride through the clouds on wild boars.

15 Friday

4th ♋
☽ v/c 5:23 pm
☽ enters ♌ 9:09 pm
Color: Pink

Set in Eastern Daylight Time (EDT)

Hāligmōnaþ (Holy Month)

After the grain harvests came to an end, the Anglo-Saxons celebrated the Holy Month (*Hāligmōnaþ*), which Saint Bede describes as "the month of offerings." By this time, the grain had been harvested and safely stored, so offerings were given to the gods in gratitude for their bounty. Straw was cut and brought in from the fields for use as thatch, basketry, and even furniture.

Hāligmōnaþ is a time of thanksgiving. Gather your coven for a traditional harvest feast. The Autumn Equinox is a favorite time for a Hāligmōnaþ feast. At least some of the food for the feast should come from your own gardens, with everyone contributing something to the meal. If you cannot do this, try to purchase fruits and vegetables from local growers. Farmers' markets are a good source for this. Local foods, whether grown yourself or by someone else, connect you with the land.

If corn (maize) is a part of your feast, save the husks and weave them into corn dollies. These can be as simple or as complex as you wish. Each person attending the feast can then take a corn dolly home and keep it on his or her altar as a reminder of the earth's many blessings.

—Alaric Albertsson

---

16 Saturday

4th ♌
Color: Gray

Passionflower is masculine, connecting to the Sun and fire. It aids sleep and brings peace.

---

17 Sunday

4th ♌
☽ v/c 8:55 pm
Color: Orange

Orange groves evoke paradise and love.

---

18 Monday

4th ♌
☽ enters ♍ 12:52 am
⚶ enters ♎ 3:50 am
Color: Ivory

19 Tuesday

4th ♍
♀ enters ♍ 9:15 pm
Color: White

A little body may harbor a great soul.

☽ Wednesday

4th ♍
☽ v/c 1:30 am
New Moon 1:30 am
☽ enters ♎ 6:06 am
Color: Topaz

21 Thursday

1st ♎
Color: Purple

Rosh Hashanah
Islamic New Year
UN International Day of Peace

22 Friday

1st ♎
☽ v/c 9:04 am
☽ enters ♏ 1:40 pm
☉ enters ♎ 4:02 pm
Color: Rose

Mabon/Fall Equinox
Sun enters Libra

Mabon

Mabon, the first day of autumn, is the main harvest and the time of the Celtic thanksgiving. It is also when the goddess Demeter lost her daughter Persephone to Hades, god of the underworld, when the women got separated while gathering flowers. Hades imprisoned Persephone in his dark world while Demeter, distraught, sought her everywhere, and the crops withered as her pain and anger grew. Finally, she went to her brother Zeus, the leader of the gods, and beseeched him to intervene. He ruled that since Persephone had eaten six pomegranate seeds while in the underworld, she would be required to stay there for six months of every year. Eventually, she came to rule the underworld along with Hades, reemerging only in spring.

Ritual ideas include enactments of the Persephone myth, complete with pomegranate seeds, to remind us of the impending "season of death." Our feasts can be full and abundant, with favorite dishes made from fresh local produce. A sweet tradition for both ritual and table can be to go around the circle and share what we're most thankful for in true thanks-giving fashion, blessing both the food and our companions with the energies of gratitude.

—Thuri Calafia

---

23 Saturday

1st ♏
Color: Blue

Gendenwitha is the Iroquois goddess of the morning star.

---

24 Sunday

1st ♏
♀ enters ♌ 1:45 am
☽ v/c 3:33 am
Color: Amber

---

25 Monday

1st ♏
☽ enters ♐ 12:01 am
Color: Lavender

26 Tuesday

1st ♐
Color: Scarlet

Eucalyptus has feminine alignment, connected with water and Venus. The oil aids concentration and balance.

◐ Wednesday

1st ♐
☽ v/c 7:08 am
☽ enters ♑ 12:24 pm
2nd quarter 10:54 pm
Color: Yellow

28 Thursday

2nd ♑
♇ D 3:36 pm
Color: Turquoise

Zlota Baba is the Slavic wealth goddess, represented by a golden statue.

29 Friday

2nd ♑
☽ v/c 8:14 pm
☿ enters ♎ 8:42 pm
Color: Coral

Tiger's Eye

Tiger's eye is a popular ornamental stone often used in carvings and jewelry. Its signature appearance of shimmering brown and gold bands is the best known, but it does occur in blue (hawk's eye) and even red (which often requires heat treatment). This eye-catching effect is called chatoyancy, a result of the mineral's interesting formation as quartz (silica) dissolves and replaces another mineral, crocidolite, which is fibrous and causes the banding.

The satiny, caramel appearance of polished tiger's eye is warm and powerful; it has a trigonal structure and is associated with the Sun and the element of fire, which is why tiger's eye is often used in spells for strength, protection, and optimism. Since tiger's eye also has strong links with the earth element, it's excellent for grounding, confidence, wealth, and good fortune.

Carry or wear tiger's eye whenever you need a boost of confidence. Charge it in full sunlight, and empower it with these words:

Stone of strength, stone of power;
I'm confident—I never cower.

—Ember Grant

---

30 Saturday

2nd ♑
☽ enters ♒ 12:40 am
Color: Black

Yom Kippur
Celtic Tree Month of Ivy begins

---

1 Sunday

2nd ♒
Color: Orange

Nicholas Drummer, an American member of the United Ancient Order, established a lodge in Paris in 1869.

October

2 Monday

2nd ≈
☽ v/c 7:13 am
☽ enters ♓ 10:26 am
Color: White

3 Tuesday

2nd ♓
Color: Red

Aha-njoku is the African goddess of yams;
she helps farmers get a good harvest.

4 Wednesday

2nd ♓
☽ v/c 3:19 am
☽ enters ♈ 4:40 pm
Color: Topaz

☺ Thursday

2nd ♈
Full Moon 2:40 pm
Color: Green

Blood Moon
Sukkot begins

6 Friday

3rd ♈
☽ v/c 6:38 pm
☽ enters ♉ 7:56 pm
Color: Rose

Set in Eastern Daylight Time (EDT)

7 Saturday

3rd ♉
Color: Blue

*The air stone jacinth increases your eloquence
and persuasion, especially when set in gold.*

8 Sunday

3rd ♉
☽ v/c 9:45 am
☽ enters ♊ 9:44 pm
Color: Gold

October

3rd ♊
Color: Lavender

Indigenous Peoples' Day

3rd ♊
♃ enters ♏ 9:20 am
☽ v/c 6:25 pm
☽ enters ♋ 11:38 pm
Color: Scarlet

3rd ♋
Color: Yellow

Sukkot ends

○ Thursday

3rd ♋
4th quarter 8:25 am
Color: Turquoise

4th ♋
☽ v/c 12:00 am
☽ enters ♌ 2:41 am
Color: Pink

*Benzoin is masculine, linked with the Sun and air. Use
it in businesses to promote prosperity and generosity.*

Winterfylleþ (Winter Full Moon)

The Full Moon in October was known to Anglo-Saxons as *Winterfylleþ* and heralded the beginning of the dark half of the year. The verb *fyllan* means "to fill," appropriate for the end of the agricultural year in northern regions and the "filling up" of the land with a new season. Today, the liminal nature of Winterfylleþ is celebrated with divinations and Halloween traditions.

Love divinations have been particularly popular both in England and the United States. The Dumb Supper was a method of love divination once practiced by young women in the Ozarks. During the ritual supper, participants expected to see visions of the men whom they would eventually marry.

Many Pagans have reclaimed the Dumb Supper as a way to commune with one's ancestors. Here the word "dumb" means mute. To hold a Dumb Supper, invite your guests to bring dishes reminding them of their ancestors and share the reason why. Then open your front door and welcome the ancestors. At this point, nobody should speak. People then eat together in silence. As you eat, listen for the words and comfort of your ancestors. When everyone is finished, end the silence by saying, "The supper is ended."

—Alaric Albertsson

---

14 Saturday

4th ♌
♀ enters ♎ 6:11 am
Color: Black

According to Egyptian tradition, black means life and rebirth.
Egypt is "the black land" because of its fertile soil.

---

15 Sunday

4th ♌
☽ v/c 1:28 am
☽ enters ♍ 7:19 am
Color: Yellow

October

16 Monday
4th ♍
Color: Silver

Palm trees represent the phallus of Osiris and
as such convey male virility and fertility

17 Tuesday
4th ♍
☿ enters ♏ 3:59 am
☽ v/c 7:27 am
☽ enters ♎ 1:35 pm
Color: White

18 Wednesday
4th ♎
Color: Brown

Crystals are selected to match the theme of
a charm or ceremony, relating to earth.

☽ Thursday
4th ♎
☽ v/c 3:12 pm
New Moon 3:12 pm
☽ enters ♏ 9:41 pm
Color: Purple

20 Friday
1st ♏
Color: Coral

Periwinkle is feminine, connected to Venus and
water. Plant on graves to help heal the loss.

Set in Eastern Daylight Time (EDT)

Witches' Stew

3 lbs. beef round steak, cubed
3 T. butter
Salt and pepper to taste
2 T. flour
16 oz. beef broth
2 cups red wine
8 oz. can tomato sauce
2 T. Worcestershire sauce
6 medium potatoes, peeled and quartered
6–8 carrots, chopped
6–8 celery stalks, chopped
1 large onion, chopped
10–12 sliced mushrooms
2 cloves garlic, pressed
2 tsp. thyme
2–3 sprigs rosemary

Fresh parsley (optional)
Bacon bits (optional)
Loaf crusty bread (optional)

In a Dutch oven over medium heat, brown beef in butter with salt and pepper to taste. When all sides are browned, add flour, stirring until beef is nice and coated. Add beef broth, wine, tomato sauce, and Worcestershire sauce. Cover and let simmer for about 1 hour. Add the rest of the ingredients (add water or more wine for a richer flavor) and let simmer another 1½ hours. Remove rosemary stems and serve with fresh parsley, bacon bits, and some crusty bread.

—Monica Crosson

---

21 Saturday

1st ♏
Color: Indigo

Blue is soothing and peaceful, an ideal color for bedrooms, bathrooms, and water altars.

---

22 Sunday

1st ♏
☽ v/c 7:35 am
☽ enters ♐ 7:57 am
♂ enters ♎ 2:29 pm
Color: Amber

October

23 Monday

1st ♐

☉ enters ♏ 1:27 am

Color: Ivory

Sun enters Scorpio

24 Tuesday

1st ♐

☽ v/c 12:44 pm

☽ enters ♑ 8:12 pm

Color: Maroon

25 Wednesday

1st ♑

Color: Yellow

Dettmer v. Landon *led to the recognition of Wicca as a religion, protected by the American Constitution, in 1985.*

26 Thursday

1st ♑

Color: Crimson

Juniper is masculine, linked with the Sun and fire. It makes spirits visible.

○ Friday

1st ♑

☽ v/c 1:22 am

☽ enters ♒ 8:59 am

2nd quarter 6:22 pm

Color: Purple

Set in Eastern Daylight Time (EDT)

Malachite

Famous for its striking green-banded patterns, malachite has long been used in carvings and jewelry. A copper carbonate mineral, it has a monoclinic structure and is associated with the planet Venus and the element of earth.

While known for transformation, malachite also has nurturing qualities. It's especially stabilizing, good for the heart chakra, and an aid for fidelity, both personal and in business—it can be good for sales. It can foster loyalty in partnerships and help one accept responsibility. So while it can be a transformative stone, it actually assists one with change rather than inducing it. It keeps you stable, gives clarity and insight to the situation, and clears the way for you to move forward.

Whether it's a change that's desired or one you can't prevent, use malachite to help you visualize the strength of the earth beneath you to help get through it. Charge the stone using this chant, and carry it with you or wear it:

In the face of change I'm able / To be calm and remain stable.
Insight and a helping hand; / Foundation firm on which to stand.

—Ember Grant

---

28 Saturday

2nd ≈
Color: Gray

Celtic Tree Month of Reed begins

---

29 Sunday

2nd ≈
☽ v/c 12:22 pm
☽ enters ♓ 7:46 pm
Color: Gold

---

30 Monday
2nd ♓
Color: Lavender

31 Tuesday
2nd ♓
☽ v/c 5:08 pm
Color: Black

Samhain/Halloween

1 Wednesday
2nd ♓
☽ enters ♈ 2:43 am
Color: Topaz

All Saints' Day

2 Thursday
2nd ♈
☽ v/c 11:03 pm
Color: White

3 Friday
2nd ♈
☽ enters ♉ 5:46 am
Color: Purple

*Wisteria is feminine, entwined with air plus Venus
and Jupiter. Use this incense for protection from evil.*

Samhain

Samhain, or Hallows' Eve, is the third harvest festival—the harvest of herbs (and the meat harvest in some traditions). The day can be a bustle of activity as gardeners try to get the crops in and bundle herbs for drying before sunset, for many Pagans consider it unlucky to pick anything once darkness falls, as it all now belongs to Hecate, the Sacred Reaper. It's a good idea to leave an offering to show reverence for our Wise Grandmother's honored role.

Samhain activities range from lighthearted celebrations, like cutting jack-o'-lanterns and dressing up to fool the spirits of the dead, to more serious rites, like the Feast for the Dead, where one sets a place for each departed loved one. Set the table with your finest dishes and reserve space for them. Make a favorite food for each of your Beloved Dead, and then serve each of them a small portion, taking your own places on the floor for just this one night to show respect for departed loved ones. Even more somber traditions include formal crossing rituals where each person speaks of those who have gone to the Summerland, chimes a bell with the uttering of each Beloved Dead's name, and lights a candle to honor each spirit.

—Thuri Calafia

☺ **Saturday**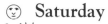

2nd ♉
Full Moon 1:23 am
Color: Black

Mourning Moon

---

5 Sunday

3rd ♉
☽ v/c 4:29 am
☽ enters ♊ 5:26 am
☿ enters ♐ 2:19 pm
Color: Yellow

Daylight Saving Time ends at 2 am

6 Monday

3rd ♊
Color: Silver

Phenacite makes wand or disk shapes; its air energy assists in major life changes and other transformations.

7 Tuesday

3rd ♊
☽ v/c 5:40 am
☽ enters ♋ 5:45 am
♀ enters ♏ 6:38 am
Color: Scarlet

Election Day (general)
Samhain crossquarter day
(Sun reaches 15° Scorpio)

8 Wednesday

3rd ♋
Color: Brown

9 Thursday

3rd ♋
☽ v/c 12:14 am
☽ enters ♌ 7:29 am
Color: Turquoise

◑ Friday

3rd ♌
4th quarter 3:36 pm
Color: Rose

Amber has masculine energy, relating to the Sun and fire. The oil is soothing and balancing.

11 Saturday

4th ♌
☽ v/c 3:55 am
☽ enters ♍ 11:41 am
Color: Gray

Veterans Day

12 Sunday

4th ♍
Color: Gold

November

13 Monday
4th ♍
☽ v/c 10:45 am
☽ enters ♎ 6:26 pm
Color: White

14 Tuesday
4th ♎
Color: Maroon

*Dragon's blood is masculine, associated with
Mars and fire. Burn it to protect your home.*

15 Wednesday
4th ♎
☽ v/c 7:50 pm
♀ enters ♈ 9:53 pm
♅ enters ♏ 11:16 pm
Color: Yellow

16 Thursday
4th ♎
☽ enters ♏ 3:19 am
Color: Green

Almond trees aid in divination and clairvoyance.

17 Friday
4th ♏
Color: Purple

Set in Eastern Standard Time (EST)

Blōdmōnaþ (Blood Month)

November was known to the Anglo-Saxon people as *Blōdmōnaþ*, or the "Blood Month." Saint Bede tells us this name was "because they sacrificed to their Gods the animals which they were about to kill." Some animals were butchered as needed throughout the year, but a new problem arose as days grew shorter and colder. The fodder put aside for winter only sustained a small percentage of the livestock over the winter. This fodder was reserved for the best breeding stock. The remaining animals were butchered throughout the Blood Month, and the meat preserved as well as possible.

Very few of us personally butcher our meat today, but you can make your own "animal" by molding a meatloaf in the shape of a cow, sheep, or hog. (Vegetarians can use bread or cookie dough.) As you consume your animal after it is baked, contemplate your own mortality and consider what you hope to accomplish in your lifetime. Be realistic, but do not be afraid to dream. Envision the web of life and how you connect with everything it touches.

This is also a time to celebrate the animals that will stay with you through the winter. Spend time with your pets and appreciate their companionship.

—Alaric Albertsson

☽ Saturday

4th ♏
☽ v/c 6:42 am
New Moon 6:42 am
☽ enters ♐ 1:59 pm
Color: Indigo

---

19 Sunday

1st ♐
Color: Amber

Motikitik is a creator god who fished the Caroline Islands out of the ocean.

November

20 Monday
1st ♐
☽ v/c 7:26 pm
Color: Ivory

*Hang a horseshoe points-up to hold luck; a smith
hangs it points-down to pour luck over the anvil.*

21 Tuesday
1st ♐
☽ enters ♑ 2:14 am
☉ enters ♐ 10:05 pm
Color: Red

Sun enters Sagittarius

22 Wednesday
1st ♑
♆ D 9:21 am
Color: White

23 Thursday
1st ♑
☽ v/c 5:33 am
☽ enters ♒ 3:14 pm
Color: Crimson

Thanksgiving Day

24 Friday
1st ♒
Color: Coral

*Candles may be of natural or synthetic wax in any
color or shape, chosen to enhance a spell or ritual.*

Topaz

Topaz occurs in nearly every color and ranges from transparent to opaque, but the mineral's pure form is colorless. The yellow-orange variety is probably the most well known, as it's the birthstone for November. It's associated with the Sun and the element of fire.

While each color of topaz has its own special properties, these are the general attributes that apply to all varieties: Metaphysically, topaz has been referred to as an especially potent mineral. It can help with motivation, allowing you to see the big picture and pave the way for manifestation. The orthorhombic crystal structure of topaz provides the added benefit of focus and perspective. Topaz also promotes individuality, encourages love and success in pursuit of goals, and can be used in spells for abundance and healing.

To put your goals into perspective and have the drive to succeed, charge your stone with these words:

Let the way be clear. / The time is finally here.
Let the outcome be / The one that's best for me.

—Ember Grant

---

25 Saturday

1st ≈
☽ v/c 9:37 pm
Color: Blue

Celtic Tree Month of Elder begins

◐ Sunday

1st ≈
☽ enters ♓ 3:04 am
2nd quarter 12:03 pm
Color: Gold

November/December

27 Monday

2nd ♓
Color: Lavender

28 Tuesday
2nd ♓
☽ v/c 7:09 am
☽ enters ♈ 11:30 am
Color: Gray

*Gotu kola is masculine, connecting to Mercury
and air. It may be burned to assist meditation.*

29 Wednesday
2nd ♈
Color: Brown

Huichaana is a Mayan creator goddess who made humanity.

30 Thursday
2nd ♈
☽ v/c 1:37 pm
☽ enters ♉ 3:38 pm
Color: Turquoise

1 Friday

2nd ♉
♀ enters ♐ 4:14 am
☽ v/c 8:53 pm
Color: Pink

Set in Eastern Standard Time (EST)

Cranberry Meatballs

2 12 oz. bags cranberries
1 cup white sugar
1 cup water
Zest of one orange
1 lb. ground beef
1 lb. sausage
Salt and pepper to taste
1 T. soy sauce
2 T. brown sugar
½ tsp. garlic powder
Hot pepper sauce to taste
1 cup brown rice

Put cranberries, white sugar, and water into a pan and cook over medium heat until glossy and thick (about 15 minutes). Add orange zest and set aside.

Mix the ground beef and sausage with salt and pepper and form into approximately 20 meatballs. Place in large skillet and cook over medium heat, turning them often to brown all sides, for 20 minutes or until cooked through. Drain off any grease from skillet and add cranberry sauce. Add soy sauce, brown sugar, garlic powder, and hot pepper sauce to taste. Turn skillet to low and let simmer about ½ hour. While meatballs are simmering, boil or steam rice. Serve the meatballs over rice.

—Monica Crosson

---

2 Saturday

2nd ♉
☽ enters ♊ 4:21 pm
Color: Blue

☺ Sunday

2nd ♊
☿ ℞ 2:34 am
Full Moon 10:47 am
Color: Amber

Long Nights Moon
Mercury retrograde until December 22

December

4 Monday

3rd ♊
☽ v/c 2:13 pm
☽ enters ♋ 3:37 pm
Color: Silver

The altar tool for water is the chalice.

5 Tuesday

3rd ♋
⚷ D 4:47 am
Color: Maroon

6 Wednesday

3rd ♋
☽ v/c 12:56 pm
☽ enters ♌ 3:37 pm
Color: White

Try camphor oil for healing, liberation,
inspiration, and purification.

7 Thursday

3rd ♌
Color: Green

Dark forest green is conservative and masculine,
a great choice for dens or altars to the God.

8 Friday

3rd ♌
☽ v/c 5:40 pm
☽ enters ♍ 6:09 pm
Color: Rose

Set in Eastern Standard Time (EST)

Ærre Geōla (Early Yule)

Early Yule (*Ærre Geōla*) is the month before the Winter Solstice. For the Anglo-Saxons, the lunar months preceding and following the solstice were both "Yule." The lack of daylight hours made practical work difficult, so the Yuletide was an ideal time for families and communities to come together in fellowship.

The solstice itself was called Mothers' Night, celebrating one's female ancestors (*idesa*). Burn rosemary at the solstice as a fragrant offering to your foremothers. As the incense burns, call out to as many of your female ancestors by name as you can, concluding with a general call to "all of the mothers who bore me."

One of the oldest of Yuletide traditions is the Yule log. This should be the largest piece of wood that fits into the hearth. Of course, many of us today do not have a fireplace, but you can burn a Yule candle. The candle custom was practiced in England as far back as the early nineteenth century. Traditional Yule candles were more than eighteen inches tall, but there is no rule for this. Light your candle at sunset on the night of the solstice. Be sure to keep a small piece of the candle later for luck through the coming year.

—Alaric Albertsson

---

9 Saturday

3rd ♍
♂ enters ♏ 3:59 am
Color: Black

◐ Sunday

3rd ♍
4th quarter 2:51 am
☽ v/c 10:02 pm
Color: Orange

Orange is flamboyant and fun. Raise your ambition with this color.

December

11 Monday
4th ♍
☽ enters ♎ 12:01 am
Color: Gray

To lift depressing thoughts or heal rifts, try neroli oil.

12 Tuesday
4th ♎
Color: Scarlet

13 Wednesday
4th ♎
☽ v/c 7:27 am
☽ enters ♏ 8:59 am
Color: Brown

Hanukkah begins

14 Thursday
4th ♏
☽ v/c 8:42 pm
Color: Turquoise

*Nephrite is a green stone with earth powers
that convey healing and prosperity.*

15 Friday
4th ♏
☽ enters ♐ 8:07 pm
Color: Coral

Set in Eastern Standard Time (EST)

16 Saturday
4th ♐
♅ enters ♒ 2:18 pm
♀ ℞ 5:28 pm
Color: Gray

17 Sunday
4th ♐
♀ D 6:36 pm
Color: Yellow

☽ Monday

4th ♐
New Moon 1:30 am
☽ v/c 8:10 am
☽ enters ♑ 8:33 am
Color: White

Jasmine is intensely feminine, corresponding to water and the Moon. This oil activates the goddess in you.

19 Tuesday

1st ♑
♄ enters ♑ 11:49 pm
Color: Red

20 Wednesday

1st ♑
☽ v/c 10:37 am
☽ enters ♒ 9:29 pm
Color: Topaz

Hanukkah ends

21 Thursday

1st ♒
☉ enters ♑ 11:28 am
Color: Crimson

Yule/Winter Solstice
Sun enters Capricorn

22 Friday

1st ♒
☿ D 8:51 pm
Color: Pink

Yule

While Samhain is the New Year for many Pagans, for others it begins at Yule with the birth of the Sun God. The Holly King passes into shadow so that the Oak King may rule this time of increase and growing light. Honor both gods in ritual by lighting the Sun God's white or gold candle from the Dark God's black one, then snuffing the black candle to symbolize the Holly King's passing.

Old traditions include bringing an evergreen tree indoors and decorating it with light and bright representations of fruit, flowers, butterflies, and birds, as well as icicle "rain" and snowflakes to show our faith that summer and abundance will come our way again.

Gift-giving is also traditional but needn't be extravagant. Gifts from the heart and homemade items often are more touching to friends and family than expensive, budget breakers. Ritual traditions can include singing or drumming up the Sun—just choose a place with a clear view of the east, and pack hot drinks and nutritious (and decadent!) snacks the night before so you can get to the chosen location before the Sun comes up. Then, sing, drum, and dance your heart out in celebration of the returning light!

—Thuri Calafia

---

23 Saturday

1st ≈
☽ v/c 5:13 am
☽ enters ♓ 9:42 am
Color: Blue

Between (Celtic Tree Month)

---

24 Sunday

1st ♓
☽ v/c 9:48 pm
Color: Gold

Christmas Eve
Celtic Tree Month of Birch begins

December

25 Monday

1st ♓

♀ enters ♑ 12:26 am
☽ enters ♈ 7:27 pm
Color: Ivory

Christmas Day

◐ Tuesday

1st ♈
2nd quarter 4:20 am
Color: White

Kwanzaa begins (ends January 1)

27 Wednesday

2nd ♈
☽ v/c 3:57 pm
Color: Yellow

28 Thursday

2nd ♈
☽ enters ♉ 1:23 am
Color: Green

29 Friday

2nd ♉
☽ v/c 9:01 am
Color: Purple

*Birch is the tree of birth, enhancing
female fertility and healthy pregnancy.*

Set in Eastern Standard Time (EST)

Rhodochrosite

Few stones can boast the stunning colors of rhodochrosite. Rhodochrosite is one of the most eye-catching minerals, ranging in tones of bright fuchsia and nearly red to pale, rosy pink and even banded with gray, white, or brown. In fact, the pink color can sometimes be so bright it looks artificial—but it's usually real. The color is due to manganese. It can even form crystals, but these are rare.

Rhodochrosite is a stone of love but has the added benefit of balance. Because it corresponds to the planet Mars and the element of fire, it's the perfect stone for drawing new love or adding a spark of renewal to a relationship.

The powerful balancing quality of the trigonal structure can stabilize emotions and offers a feeling of calm acceptance. Rhodochrosite can also be used in earth-healing rituals and to gain access to one's higher self.

Charge rhodochrosite in sunlight and create a love talisman to carry with you. Visualize your need and chant,

> *Love like fire, burn hotter, burn higher; / Familiar or new, let love inspire.*
> *Balance in love, respect and desire— / Love in all forms, accept and admire.*
> —Ember Grant

---

30 Saturday

2nd ♉
☽ enters ♊ 3:31 am
Color: Indigo

Eat black-eyed peas on New Year's
Eve for prosperity during the year.

---

31 Sunday

2nd ♊
☽ v/c 6:38 pm
Color: Orange

New Year's Eve

About the Authors

ALARIC ALBERTSSON is the author of several books published by Llewellyn, including *Travels Through Middle Earth: The Path of a Saxon Pagan* and *Wyrdworking: The Path of a Saxon Sorcerer*. A follower of the Old Ways since 1971, his personal spiritual practice is a synthesis of Anglo-Saxon tradition, herbal studies, and rune lore. In the 1990s, he served on the board of directors of the Heartland Spiritual Alliance. Over the years he has worn many hats: gardener, massage therapist, beekeeper, teacher, and writer. Alaric lives in western Pennsylvania and can be contacted through his website at www.alaricalbertsson.com.

ELIZABETH BARRETTE was the managing editor of *PanGaia* and has been involved with the Pagan community for twenty-five years, actively networking via coffeehouse meetings and open sabbats. Her other writings include speculative fiction and gender studies. Her book *Composing Magic* explains how to write spells, rituals, and other liturgy. She lives in central Illinois and enjoys herbal landscaping and gardening for wildlife. Visit www.penultimate productions.weebly.com.

MONICA CROSSON is a Master Gardener who lives in the beautiful Pacific Northwest, happily digging in the dirt and tending her raspberries with her husband, three kids, three goats, one dog, three cats, a dozen chickens, and Rosetta the donkey. She has been a practicing Witch for twenty years and is a member of Blue Moon Coven. Monica writes fiction for young adults and is the author of *Summer Sage*. Visit her website at www.monicacrosson.com.

THURI CALAFIA is the author of *Dedicant: A Witch's Circle of Fire* and *Initiate: A Witch's Circle of Water* and is busy finishing up the third Circles series book, *Adept: A Witch's Circle of Earth*. She is an ordained minister and Wiccan High Priestess, teacher, and creator of the Circles system and Circles School. She lives in the Pacific Northwest with her Labrador, Briana Fae.

ELLEN DUGAN is the award-winning author of seventeen metaphysical non-fiction books. She branched out into fiction with her first paranormal series, Legacy of Magick. Ellen lives an enchanted life in Missouri. Visit her website at www.ellendugan.com.

KATHLEEN EDWARDS sold her first artworks in sixth grade—drawings of peace signs and flowers for ten cents each. She's been a book illustrator since 1991, and her work includes many Llewellyn publications. Her award-winning fine-art paintings have been widely exhibited and her graphic book, *Holy Stars!: Favorite Deities, Prophets, Saints & Sages from Around the World*, was published in 2009. See more of her work at www.kathleenedwardsartist.com.

EMBER GRANT is the author of *Magical Candle Crafting*, *The Book of Crystal Spells*, and *The Second Book of Crystal Spells*, and she has been writing for the Llewellyn annuals since 2003. She enjoys nature photography, gardening, and making candles, soap, cards, and jewelry. Visit her at www.embergrant.com.

ROBIN IVY PAYTON is the yoga intuitive of Portland, Maine. Astrologer for *The Portland Phoenix* and *Robin's Zodiac Zone*, Robin also writes about yoga, meditation, health, and the powers of music, color, and nature. A yoga and meditation teacher, Robin created RoZoYo®, her fusion of astrology and yoga. She teaches in the Portland, Maine, area and at festivals such as Love Yoga Fest in Hyannis, Massachusetts. Robin appears on radio broadcasts including *Ultrasounds* on WMNF in Tampa, Florida.

SUZANNE RESS earned an MA from Johns Hopkins University and has been writing for many years. Her first novel, *The Trial of Goody Gilbert*, was published in 2012. She has since completed two more, as yet unpublished, novels and has begun working on a fourth. She is an organic farmer and beekeeper and lives in the foothills of the Italian Alps with her husband and many domestic and wild animals.

CHARLIE RAINBOW WOLF is happiest when she is creating something, especially if it can be made from items that others have cast aside. Pottery, writing, knitting, astrology, and tarot are her deepest interests, but she happily confesses that she's easily distracted because life offers so many wonderful things to explore. She is an advocate of organic gardening and cooking and lives in the Midwest with her husband and special-needs Great Danes. Visit www.charlierainbow.com.

Appendix

Daily Magical Influences

Each day is ruled by a planet with specific magical influences.

Monday (Moon): peace, healing, caring, psychic awareness
Tuesday (Mars): passion, courage, aggression, protection
Wednesday (Mercury): study, travel, divination, wisdom
Thursday (Jupiter): expansion, money, prosperity, generosity
Friday (Venus): love, friendship, reconciliation, beauty
Saturday (Saturn): longevity, endings, homes
Sunday (Sun): healing, spirituality, success, strength, protection

Color Correspondences

Colors are associated with each day, according to planetary influence.

Monday: gray, lavender, white, silver, ivory
Tuesday: red, white, black, gray, maroon, scarlet
Wednesday: yellow, brown, white, topaz
Thursday: green, turquoise, white, purple, crimson
Friday: white, pink, rose, purple, coral
Saturday: brown, gray, blue, indigo, black
Sunday: yellow, orange, gold, amber

Lunar Phases

Waxing, from New Moon to Full Moon, is the ideal time to do magic to draw things to you.

Waning, from Full Moon to New Moon, is a time for study, meditation, and magical work designed to banish harmful energies.

The Moon's Sign

The Moon continuously moves through each sign of the zodiac, from Aries to Pisces, staying about two and a half days in each sign. The Moon influences the sign it inhabits, creating different energies that affect our day-to-day lives.

Aries: Good for starting things. Things occur rapidly but quickly pass. People tend to be argumentative and assertive.

Taurus: Things begun now last longest, tend to increase in value, and become hard to change. Brings out an appreciation for beauty and sensory experience.

Gemini: Things begun now are easily changed by outside influence. Time for shortcuts, communication, games, and fun.

Cancer: Stimulates emotional rapport between people. Supports growth and nurturing. Tend to domestic concerns.

Leo: Draws emphasis to the self, to central ideas or institutions, away from connections with others and emotional needs.

Virgo: Favors accomplishment of details and commands from higher up. Focus on health, hygiene, and daily schedules.

Libra: Favors cooperation, compromise, social activities, balance, friendship, and partnership.

Scorpio: Increases awareness of psychic power. Precipitates psychic crises and ends connections thoroughly. People have a tendency to brood and become secretive.

Sagittarius: Encourages confidence and flights of imagination. This is an adventurous, philosophical, and athletic Moon sign. Favors expansion and growth.

Capricorn: Develops strong structure. Focus on traditions, responsibilities, and obligations. A good time to set boundaries and rules.

Aquarius: Rebellious energy. Time to break habits and make abrupt change. Personal freedom and individuality is the focus.

Pisces: The focus is on dreaming, nostalgia, intuition, and psychic impressions. A good time for spiritual or philanthropic activities.

2017 Eclipses

February 10, 7:44 pm; Lunar eclipse 22° ♌ 28'
February 26, 9:54 am; Solar eclipse 8° ♓ 12'
August 7, 2:21 pm; Lunar eclipse 15° ♒ 25'
August 21, 2:25 pm; Solar eclipse 28° ♌ 53'

2017 Full Moons

Cold Moon: January 12, 6:43 am
Quickening Moon: February 10, 7:33 pm
Storm Moon: March 12, 10:54 am
Wind Moon: April 11, 2:08 am
Flower Moon: May 10, 5:42 pm
Strong Sun Moon: June 9, 9:10 am
Blessing Moon: July 9, 12:07 am
Corn Moon: August 7, 2:11 pm
Harvest Moon: September 6, 3:03 am
Blood Moon: October 5, 2:40 pm
Mourning Moon: November 4, 1:23 am
Long Nights Moon: December 3, 10:47 am

Planetary Retrogrades in 2017

Planet		Retrograde			Direct	
Mercury	℞	12/19/16	5:55 am	— Direct	01/08/17	4:43 am
Jupiter	℞	02/06/17	1:52 am	— Direct	06/09/17	10:03 am
Venus	℞	03/04/17	4:09 am	— Direct	04/15/17	6:18 am
Saturn	℞	04/06/17	1:06 am	— Direct	08/25/17	8:08 am
Mercury	℞	04/09/17	7:14 pm	— Direct	05/03/17	12:33 pm
Pluto	℞	04/20/17	8:49 am	— Direct	09/28/17	3:36 pm
Neptune	℞	06/16/17	7:09 am	— Direct	11/22/17	9:21 am
Uranus	℞	08/03/17	1:31 am	— Direct	01/02/18	9:13 am
Mercury	℞	08/12/17	9:00 pm	— Direct	09/05/17	7:29 am
Mercury	℞	12/03/17	2:34 am	— Direct	12/22/17	8:51 pm

Set in Eastern Time. All times corrected for Daylight Saving Time.

Moon Void-of-Course Data for 2017

JANUARY

Last Aspect Date	Time	New Sign	New Time
2	2:59 am	2 ♓	4:57 am
4	11:14 am	4 ♈	11:20 am
6	1:41 pm	6 ♉	3:18 pm
7	9:23 pm	8 ♊	5:06 pm
10	4:38 pm	10 ♋	5:49 pm
12	6:34 am	12 ♌	7:08 pm
14	10:17 am	14 ♍	10:52 pm
17	1:09 am	17 ♎	6:16 am
19	3:55 am	19 ♏	5:09 pm
21	8:24 pm	22 ♐	5:45 am
24	12:33 pm	24 ♑	5:43 pm
27	2:18 am	27 ♒	3:37 am
29	12:52 am	29 ♓	11:10 am
31	12:36 pm	31 ♈	4:46 am

FEBRUARY

Last Aspect Date	Time	New Sign	New Time
2	11:50 am	2 ♉	8:50 pm
4	5:42 pm	4 ♊	11:44 pm
6	5:53 pm	7 ♋	2:03 am
8	5:00 pm	9 ♌	4:41 am
11	12:52 am	11 ♍	8:52 am
13	7:36 am	13 ♎	3:43 pm
15	8:54 pm	16 ♏	1:41 am
17	2:38 pm	18 ♐	1:52 pm
20	6:37 pm	21 ♑	2:08 am
22	10:24 pm	23 ♒	12:17 pm
25	1:11 pm	25 ♓	7:24 pm
27	6:08 pm	27 ♈	11:52 pm

MARCH

Last Aspect Date	Time	New Sign	New Time
1	9:18 pm	2 ♉	2:43 am
3	10:20 am	4 ♊	5:05 am
6	3:22 am	6 ♋	7:54 am
8	9:59 am	8 ♌	11:45 am
10	12:06 pm	10 ♍	5:07 pm
12	10:36 pm	13 ♎	1:28 am
15	6:05 am	15 ♏	11:11 am
17	5:56 pm	17 ♐	11:00 pm
20	6:37 am	20 ♑	11:31 am
22	9:20 am	22 ♒	10:28 pm
25	1:56 am	25 ♓	6:06 am
27	6:19 am	27 ♈	10:11 am
29	8:07 am	29 ♉	11:48 am
30	7:12 pm	31 ♊	12:40 pm

APRIL

Last Aspect Date	Time	New Sign	New Time
2	10:43 am	2 ♋	2:27 pm
4	4:45 pm	4 ♌	6:13 pm
6	8:16 pm	7 ♍	12:20 am
9	4:21 pm	9 ♎	8:34 am
11	2:19 pm	11 ♏	6:42 pm
14	12:18 am	14 ♐	6:27 am
16	2:26 pm	16 ♑	7:05 pm
19	5:57 am	19 ♒	6:52 am
21	2:23 pm	21 ♓	3:43 pm
23	5:34 pm	23 ♈	8:32 pm
25	5:53 pm	25 ♉	9:56 pm
27	9:18 pm	27 ♊	9:39 pm
29	5:28 pm	29 ♋	9:48 pm

MAY

Last Aspect Date	Time	New Sign	New Time
1	4:23 pm	2 ♌	12:12 am
4	12:35 am	4 ♍	5:47 am
6	8:42 am	6 ♎	2:20 pm
8	6:59 pm	9 ♏	1:01 am
10	5:42 pm	11 ♐	12:59 pm
13	10:14 pm	14 ♑	1:37 am
16	6:22 am	16 ♒	1:50 pm
18	8:33 pm	18 ♓	11:52 pm
20	11:39 pm	21 ♈	6:10 am
23	2:59 am	23 ♉	8:33 am
24	3:08 pm	25 ♊	8:15 am
27	2:18 am	27 ♋	7:25 am
29	2:59 am	29 ♌	8:12 am
31	7:14 am	31 ♍	12:16 pm

JUNE

Last Aspect Date	Time	New Sign	New Time
2	5:48 pm	2 ♎	8:04 pm
5	4:57 am	5 ♏	6:46 am
6	8:35 pm	7 ♐	6:59 pm
10	2:20 am	10 ♑	7:36 am
12	2:45 pm	12 ♒	7:45 pm
15	1:40 am	15 ♓	6:17 am
17	7:33 am	17 ♈	1:55 pm
19	3:42 pm	19 ♉	5:53 pm
21	12:26 am	21 ♊	6:44 pm
23	2:45 pm	23 ♋	6:07 pm
25	2:44 pm	25 ♌	6:06 pm
27	5:12 pm	27 ♍	8:41 pm
29	4:35 pm	30 ♎	3:02 am

JULY

Last Aspect Date	Time	New Sign	New Time
2	9:16 am	2 ♏	12:59 pm
4	9:34 am	5 ♐	1:08 am
7	10:12 am	7 ♑	1:45 pm
9	10:12 pm	10 ♒	1:35 am
12	8:40 am	12 ♓	11:51 am
14	1:00 pm	14 ♈	7:52 pm
16	10:19 pm	17 ♉	1:04 am
19	2:11 am	19 ♊	3:31 am
21	1:41 am	21 ♋	4:09 am
23	2:05 am	23 ♌	4:34 am
25	5:22 am	25 ♍	6:32 am
27	2:31 am	27 ♎	11:37 am
29	5:30 pm	29 ♏	8:23 pm
31	7:10 am	8/1 ♐	8:01 am

AUGUST

Last Aspect Date	Time	New Sign	New Time
7/31	7:10 am	1 ♐	8:01 am
3	5:38 pm	3 ♑	8:37 pm
6	5:22 am	6 ♒	8:15 am
8	3:07 pm	8 ♓	5:56 pm
10	9:38 am	11 ♈	1:22 am
13	4:01 am	13 ♉	6:40 am
15	9:15 am	15 ♊	10:06 am
17	9:38 am	17 ♋	12:13 pm
19	11:17 am	19 ♌	1:55 pm
21	2:30 pm	21 ♍	4:25 pm
23	4:02 pm	23 ♎	9:05 pm
26	1:39 am	26 ♏	4:53 am
28	5:38 am	28 ♐	3:48 pm
31	12:42 am	31 ♑	4:18 am

SEPTEMBER

Last Aspect Date	Time	New Sign	New Time
2	12:30 pm	2 ♒	4:06 pm
5	1:15 am	5 ♓	1:28 am
6	4:29 pm	7 ♈	8:01 am
9	11:52 am	9 ♉	12:23 pm
10	8:54 pm	11 ♊	3:29 pm
13	2:35 pm	13 ♋	6:12 pm
15	5:23 pm	15 ♌	9:09 pm
17	8:55 pm	18 ♍	12:52 am
20	1:30 am	20 ♎	6:06 am
22	9:04 am	22 ♏	1:40 pm
24	3:33 am	25 ♐	12:01 am
27	7:08 am	27 ♑	12:24 pm
29	8:14 pm	30 ♒	12:40 am

OCTOBER

Last Aspect Date	Time	New Sign	New Time
2	7:13 am	2 ♓	10:26 am
4	3:19 am	4 ♈	4:40 pm
6	6:38 pm	6 ♉	7:56 pm
8	9:45 am	8 ♊	9:44 pm
10	6:25 pm	10 ♋	11:38 pm
13	12:00 am	13 ♌	2:41 am
15	1:28 am	15 ♍	7:19 am
17	7:27 am	17 ♎	1:35 pm
19	3:12 pm	19 ♏	9:41 pm
22	7:35 am	22 ♐	7:57 am
24	12:44 pm	24 ♑	8:12 pm
27	1:22 am	27 ♒	8:59 am
29	12:22 pm	29 ♓	7:46 pm
31	5:08 pm	11/1 ♈	2:43 am

NOVEMBER

Last Aspect Date	Time	New Sign	New Time
10/31	5:08 pm	1 ♈	2:43 am
2	11:03 pm	3 ♉	5:46 am
5	4:29 am	5 ♊	5:26 am
7	5:40 am	7 ♋	5:45 am
9	12:14 am	9 ♌	7:29 am
11	3:55 pm	11 ♍	11:41 am
13	10:45 am	13 ♎	6:26 pm
15	7:50 pm	16 ♏	3:19 am
18	6:42 am	18 ♐	1:59 pm
20	7:26 pm	21 ♑	2:14 am
23	5:33 am	23 ♒	3:14 pm
25	9:37 pm	26 ♓	3:04 am
28	7:09 am	28 ♈	11:30 am
30	1:37 pm	30 ♉	3:38 pm

DECEMBER

Last Aspect Date	Time	New Sign	New Time
1	8:53 pm	2 ♊	4:21 pm
4	2:13 pm	4 ♋	3:37 pm
6	12:56 pm	6 ♌	3:37 pm
8	5:40 pm	8 ♍	6:09 pm
10	10:02 pm	11 ♎	12:01 am
13	7:27 am	13 ♏	8:59 am
14	8:42 pm	15 ♐	8:07 pm
18	8:10 am	18 ♑	8:33 am
20	10:37 am	20 ♒	9:29 pm
23	5:13 am	23 ♓	9:42 am
24	9:48 pm	25 ♈	7:27 pm
27	3:57 pm	28 ♉	1:23 am
29	9:01 pm	30 ♊	3:31 am
31	6:38 pm	1/1 ♋	3:10 am

Set in Eastern Time. All times corrected for Daylight Saving Time.

Practical Ideas for Enhancing Your Craft

Llewellyn's *Magical Almanac* has been inspiring all levels of magical practitioners for over twenty years. It is filled with practical spells, rituals, and fresh ideas, and you'll find new ways to deepen your craft and enhance everyday life.

This edition features compelling articles on magic for travel and for city life, animal apantomancy, psychometry, empathy and magic, shamanic careers, labyrinth spells, healing with Himalayan salt, and much more. Also included is a calendar section featuring world festivals, holidays, astrological information, incense and color correspondences, and 2017 sabbats.

**LLEWELLYN'S 2017
MAGICAL ALMANAC**
336 pp. • 5¼ x 8
978-0-7387-3762-1 • U.S. $11.99 Can $14.99
To order call 1-877-NEW-WRLD
www.llewellyn.com

Meditations Spells, and Rituals for Every Day

Make every day magical with a spell from *Llewellyn's Witches' Spell-A-Day Almanac*. Spellcasters of all levels can enhance their daily life with these easy bewitchments, recipes, rituals, and meditations.

James Kambos, Barbara Ardinger, Deborah Blake, and other experienced magic practitioners offer simple spells for every occasion. For convenience, the 365 spells are cross-referenced by purpose: love, health, money, protection, home and garden, travel, and communication. Beginners will find advice on the best time, place, and tools to perform each spell. With space to jot down notes, this unique spellbook can be used as a Book of Shadows.

Notes

Notes

Notes